Make It Memorable

Also by Robyn Freedman Spizman

The Giftionary

Make It Memorable

An A-to-Z Guide
to Making Any Event,
Gift, or Occasion . . .
Dazzling!

Robyn Freedman Spizman

St. Martin's Griffin 🐾 New York

This book is dedicated to my readers.
May you make life as meaningful as possible
and live in such a way that your actions and deeds
forever reside in the hearts of others.

www.stmartins.com

Design by RLF Design

Library of Congress Cataloging-in-Publication Data

Spizman, Robyn Freedman.
    Make it memorable! : an A-to-Z guide to making any event, gift, or occasion—dazzling! / Robyn Freedman Spizman.—1st ed.
      p. cm.
    ISBN 0-312-32846-X
    EAN 978-0312-32846-7
    1. Special events—Planning. 2. Gifts—Planning. I. Title.

GT3045.S65 2004
394.2—dc22

                                                              2004048053

First Edition: October 2004

10 9 8 7 6 5 4 3 2 1

Contents

Acknowledgments

My heartfelt appreciation goes to the most precious gifts in my life—my family and friends. To Willy, my wonderful husband, who read this book word for word: your endless love and support sustain me. To our best gifts ever—our children, Justin and Ali—your precious presence makes my life totally worthwhile and increasingly memorable. To my devoted parents, Phyllis and Jack Freedman, for their endless gifts of wisdom, and a lifetime of unconditional love. Thank you to my brother Doug and his real-life Genie, to Sam and Gena (hurray!), Aunt Lois and Uncle Jerry Blonder, Aunt Ramona Freedman, and to my entire family; my heartfelt thanks for all the treasured memories, past and present. To my beloved grandparents, and family who are no longer present, you will forever be close to my heart. And to Bettye Storne, my devoted friend and real-life angel. You are all the very best gifts life has to offer!

To my dedicated literary agent and friend, with a signature style all her own—Meredith Bernstein—thank you for your unwavering friendship and unending confidence. To St. Martin's Most Memorable: Matthew Shear (Publisher Extraordinaire), Jennifer Enderlin (the finest editor anyone could ask to work with), John Karle and Sarah Cocroft (the ultimate publicists—way to glow!), and Kimberly Cardascia, Meryl Gross, and Michael Storrings for your wonderful help. To the talented Paige Janco and Suzi Brozman, for your continued assistance, and to the Spizman Agency—your creative and ongoing support is immeasurable.

To my remarkable and talented friend Jack Morton (who I so adore!), and his special staff at Indulgence Salon, for keeping a smile on my face and my hair in place. To *Women for Hire* career-fair guru, Tory Johnson, my truly gifted friend and shopping diva, and her devoted staff. My ongoing thanks to PTA's extraordinary Rick Frishman, the amazing and dedicated Hillary Rivman, and Kristin Clifford. To my television "Been There Bought That" best buddies for life, Tiffany Cochran, and the team that makes us all look great, the dedicated Kalina "Elmo" Haynes, Holly Short, Cal Callaway, Annika Young, Ann Shelton, Jayne McClinton, Jill Becker, Karyn Greer, and everyone at WXIA-TV 11 Alive. And to the shining stars at Star 94: Mark Kanov, who believed in my book *The Giftionary* and teamed me up with Cindy Simmons, Ray Mariner and Kristen Gates (Atlanta's gifts to radio—I am your biggest fan!), and to the talented and wonderful Nancy Joffre—I adore you all! Plus, a heartfelt thanks also goes to three remarkable individuals who are positively life's best examples in the big-time world at work: Joanne LaMarca, Betsy Alexander, and Mary Lynn Ryan.

To Steven M. Winter, and Doug Isenberg, for your expert advice, and to my extended family, circle of friends, and contributors to this book, who have my endless thanks, including: Patty and Larry Brown, Gail and Lyons Heyman, Carla and Ralph Lovell, Linda and Howard Reisman, Lorie Lewis and Les Fuchs, Ava and Bob Wilensky, Betty and Alan Sunshine, Lori and Arthur Simon, Nancy and Wayne Freedman, Norma and Peter Gordon, Donna and Michael Weinstock, Shirley and Barry Retter, Terry and Herb Spector, Marianne and Stephen Garber, Laurie Selzer, Marla Shavin, Terri Zieve, Viki Freeman, Janie Fishman, AvivA Hoffmann, Cheryl Isaacs, Lisa Karesh, JacLynn and Bruce Morris, Wendy Light, Susan Silber, Phyllis Rosenberg, The Helens, Ellen Banov, my Margaret Mitchell Buds, Rosemary and H. Jackson Brown Jr., Mark Victor Hansen, Stedman Graham, Lindsay Roberts, Leslie Isenberg, Dale and Jeff Dyer, The Blonders, Bruce T. Blythe, Harriette Bawarsky, The Hoffmans, The Stryers, The Gossens, The Cohens, The Freedmans, Deedee Chereton, Fay and Donald Gold, Denise Rindsberg, The Fritz Family, Jamie Finkel, Anita Goodman, Narvie Harris, Tracy Green, Keith Saxe, The Alpers, The Sturms, Dr. David Garber, Dr. Ronald Goldstein, Barbara Cochran Berry, The Madsons, Sherry Halpern, Abby and Joyce Slotin, Cari Wira, Susan Einsenstein, Melanie Morton, Diane Smith, Richard Rubin, Evelyn Mims, Carly Heyman, Lynne Halpern, Katy Schreiner, Marci Spatz, Faye Ivanova, Bette Dickson, Theresa Sutton, Sandy Abrams, Joan Weiss, Dr. Jim Braude, Emily Reed, Diane Caldwell, Alice Hicks, Mike Hughes, Pete

Wilkerson, Sylvia Weinstock, Tony Conway, Sue Winner, Joni Alpert, Kathy Alonso, Amanda Perkins, Beverly Sears, Ryan McEntyre, Varda Sauer, Diane Burton-Maroney, Margaret Lawson, Andrew Saltzman, Anne Dennington, Kimberly Segale, Marcy Solmson, Cara Lamb, Mitzi Kahn, Allen Hardin, Bo and Sheri Hardin, Maggie Hasbrouck, Rebecca Carter, Betti Mori, Oscar Culp, Gail Evans, Gwen Ware of the Electronic Pencil, Leigh Forrester, Gwen Bloom, Seth and Wendy Goldberg, Barbara Kaufman, Ed Chapman, Angela Hylenski, Alison Peppers, Dee Seeds, Pat Harmon, Cindy Robbins, Laura Weiss, Edie and the beloved Ben Lehrner, Josh Weinstock, Roxanne Housley, Dr. Dan Baker, Katie Garber, Bonnie Marson, and the many individuals who have supported and inspired me throughout the years.

And on a final note, to the many readers who have read and shared my books for decades, you honor me with your continued presence.

*Life is not measured
by the number of breaths we take,
but the moments that take
our breath away.*

—Author unknown

Introduction

For some individuals, creating memorable moments comes easily, but for most, a little creative SOS provides welcome relief! When you create a lasting memory, you enter someone's heart, and then capture their mind and imagination. In some way, your deed or action becomes immortal, and inspires grateful thoughts in the memory of the receiver throughout time. Memories are the links in our lives that keep us connected, and remind us of those treasured moments shared with loved ones that deeply touched us. They allow us the luxury of replaying those times when we have felt most loved, comforted, and cherished.

When I think of my fondest memories, I instantly recall the many dinners spent with my family, the platters of delicious cookies that my Grandma Annie lovingly baked, and the cupcakes with pink icing and little candy hearts on Valentine's morning. I can hear my parents' voices telling me they love me. I can recall the moment my husband and I were told we were the proud parents of a baby boy, who we named Justin, and then, six years later, a beautiful baby girl we named Ali. While there are endless other memories I think of often, I especially remember the perfect day my husband gave me one Mother's Day, when my every wish was his command. Those little treasured deeds, along with a lifetime of memorable moments, have become the bookmarks of my life, and they fill my heart with gladness, and inspire me to make life's special moments memorable for others.

It's interesting to see what ultimately becomes memorable, but comedian Bob Hope captured it best in his familiar tune, "Thanks for the Memories"! He dedicated many of his one hundred years to singing that sentimental song, and left a legacy that touched millions of people. Memories are clearly the moments in time we selectively preserve and store in our hearts. The memories of our actions and deeds reward our efforts, and embed us in the lives of others forever. These memories then motivate us to perpetuate them, making them a significant part of how we celebrate our relationships, both past and present.

In my book, *The Giftionary: An A–Z Reference Guide For Solving Your Gift Giving Dilemmas . . . Forever!*, I wrote about the manner in which a gift should be given. In *When Words Matter Most,* I celebrated the power of words, and in *The Thank You Book,* I acknowledged the importance of saying "thank you." Now, in the tradition of celebrating what I believe makes life so very special, I'll continue to help you embrace the days of your life, and express your feelings for those you care about in intensely significant ways. My hope is to help you sign your deeds and actions with flair, and develop a signature style all your own—to help you touch someone, and make a difference, so that your efforts stick in their minds and hearts forever.

Consider for a moment an occasion you hold near and dear to your heart. What made it so impressive? What was it about that single occurrence, when time stood still? Did someone make you feel like a hero? Were you invited to a party filled with sentiment that moved you? Did you attend a ceremony that touched you forever? Or, did someone make you feel so adored and cherished, you felt genuinely loved?

As the gatekeepers of our hearts, we recognize the need for making memories and then freezing them in time. Those really precious ones are never lost as we turn them to gold. Through both happy and sad times, we define our lives by those memorable thoughts and actions that inspire us to live a deeper life of meaning and purpose. And in memory of loved ones near and dear to our hearts, we also discover the importance of passing down their traditions and actions, while making the most of every moment.

Throughout the years, I have discovered that true wealth comes from the unparalleled blessings of those moments that leave us awestruck and take our breath away. They are more precious than jewels, and become life's greatest rewards when we capture them and pass them on.

I've always said I write books so that I can live forever, but the truth is we can all live forever in the hearts of those around us by spreading small acts of kindness that leave a gentle reminder that we graced the earth, and brightened our corner of it. It is my hope that the ideas in this book will serve as a reminder that you, too, can make every moment memorable, and life more meaningful along the way.

Make it memorable!

—*Robyn Freedman Spizman*

Life itself cannot give you joy,

Unless you really will it.

Life just gives you time and space,

It's up to you to fill it.

—Chinese Proverb

𝒜

is for Awesome Anniversaries

I t has been said throughout time that love is symbolically the gift of oneself. Wrapped with affection, it's a gift expressed by your attention, appreciation, and total adoration for another person. As each anniversary approaches, from the moment you met, this special day that's marked in time is Cupid's wake-up call to remind you to express your love and concern and, of course, make it memorable.

A wedding anniversary is a wonderful time to reflect on special memories and that momentous day when someone you care about (perhaps even you) said, "I do." Besides the traditional anniversary of a marriage, there are also many other anniversaries, ranging from the anniversary of the day you met, to your very first date. An anniversary is not just a time to acknowledge memories past, rather it's also a time to create new memories, and celebrate someone you care about, and that special day.

Some anniversaries fly by unnoticed, while others are totally embedded in your heart as a spectacular moment in time. Your goal is to mark the occasion with a token of your affection that makes your partner, or a couple you wish to congratulate, feel totally adored. Since that's easier said than done, I interviewed hundreds of people to find a few of the most meaningful anniversaries ever.

Anniversary Gifts By Years

Stick To Tradition ☺ If you're a stickler for tradition, then the following list will help you choose gifts that suit the occasion. However, to be memorable, you have to get out of the (gift) box, and add an experience to your gift that transforms it. The first anniversary might be paper, but that also means a love letter (they always work), plane tickets back to your honeymoon resort, the deed to a new house, the lease to a new car, hundreds of Post-it notes covering the bathroom mirror that say "I Love You," and more. Don't just rely on the tried-and-true, get creative, and add the fun back in to gift-giving!

Year	Traditional	Modern
1st	Paper, plastic	Clock
2nd	Cotton	China
3rd	Leather	Crystal, glass
4th	Linen, silk, flowers, fruit	Appliances
5th	Wood	Silverware
6th	Candy, iron	Wood
7th	Copper, wool	Desk sets
8th	Bronze, pottery	Linens, lace
9th	Pottery, willow	Leather, china, glass
10th	Tin, aluminum	Diamond jewelry
11th	Steel	Fashion jewelry
12th	Linen, silk	Pearls, nylon
13th	Lace	Furs, textiles
14th	Ivory	Gold jewelry
15th	Crystal, glass	Watch
20th	China	Platinum
25th	Silver	Silver
30th	Pearl	Diamond jewelry
35th	Jade, coral	Jade
40th	Ruby, garnet	Ruby
45th	Sapphire	Sapphire
50th	Gold	Gold
55th	Emerald, turquoise	Emerald
60th	Diamond	Diamond or gold
75th	Diamond	Diamond

Create An Anniversary Time Line © From the moment they met to their big anniversary celebration, create a time line of special events, moments in their shared lives, funny details as well, and include all the meaningful and momentous events you can uncover from friends and family. Give out the time line on pretty cards and frame an enlarged version for the anniversary couple. This will be a wonderful gift that captures forgotten memories past.

Capture The Moment © Sylvia Weinstock, one of the most famous cake designers in New York City, shared one of her most meaningful gifts, one she gave a couple for their thirty-fifth wedding anniversary. The host had made a little speech at the party about his bride that was very touching. Inspired, Sylvia managed to get an exact copy, and had the speech scripted in calligraphy. She then had the speech framed and sent it to them as a gift. The couple had everything already, but this gift became a priceless treasure.

A Girl Named Maureen © Here's a touching anniversary celebration Jennifer Enderlin and her siblings arranged on the occasion of her parents' fortieth wedding anniversary. She coordinated all the plans, with a detailed itinerary, for a trip to Arizona on their anniversary weekend. Her brothers and sisters all pitched in by sending bottles of champagne and other thoughtful gifts to their hotel. To make it really memorable, though, she and her siblings scoured through letters written by their father to his parents, over forty years ago, announcing that he had met a girl named Maureen. Each of the siblings included passages from these prized letters in their greeting cards, and marked the moment their parents met with memories from the past. The cards were all marked, "Do not open until October 23rd."

Indulgences Galore © Anniversaries are a time to create new memories. On your anniversary day, whisk your partner off to a day of indulgences. Rent that car you have always had your heart set on, and take a drive into the country and back. Or, head to a nearby bed-and-breakfast, or inn, for a twenty-four-hour getaway. Request that the inn cover the bed in rose petals, and provide a bottle of champagne and strawberries for dessert. Inquire what other services they can offer to make your stay memorable, and plan ahead for a romantic interlude.

Is There Anything Else You Want? © Here's a memorable tradition that Andrew Saltzman follows on his wedding anniversary every year: when he selects a gift for his wife, he gives it with an "anything you want" guarantee and the condition that she has to go and see if there's anything else she'd rather have. Two points, Andrew! I thought that was a really memorable way to give a gift to insure happiness and, just in case, this allows his wife to make sure there's no other gift she'd rather have.

If Life's A Game © Transform a game board into a lasting work of art by spelling out your love for her (or him) with letters from the game of Scrabble. Glue the tiles to the board permanently, and score points with phrases like, "I love you forever" or, "Will you marry me again?" Get creative, and give her the game with your sentiment inside. You're bound to cast a spell over her with this creative display of your affection. The game board can also be framed as a keepsake to preserve the moment.

Shower Them With Affection © Do a little research and create an actual themed wedding shower. That's right. Throw an actual shower even though the couple has been married twenty-five years. Inquire what their favorite party or memory was from their wedding, and then recreate it. Guests can bring gifts or, in lieu of gifts, invite friends and family members to bring their favorite memory of the couple. All of the entrances can be put in a scrapbook for a treasured keepsake.

Light Up Her Life © Every year, even if you have plans to go out to dinner, have a special anniversary celebration at home to show how you are the light of each other's lives. Securely place a candle in a special empty bottle, and designate it as your anniversary bottle. You might even use the bottle of champagne you shared when you got engaged. Light the candle, and let the candle wax drip down on the bottle as you eat. Each year, use a different colored candle in the bottle. This can become a tradition, and you can look back at the layers and remember every special year together.

Cruising Along © Recreate their anniversary cruise with a Love Boat party theme focused on the same ship they cruised on their anniversary. For example, if they cruised on the Emerald Seas, and went to the Bahamas, do a little research, and re-create that big buffet, unlimited desserts, and throw a dinner party with suitcase centerpieces, and an evening of fun, and festivities. Hang signs that say, "Welcome to The _____ Love Boat. All aboard for a good time down memory lane." Request that guests bring a memory to share, and fill a wedding scrapbook with these memories as a wonderful keepsake.

The Book Of Love ◎ Designate a special book as your "love book." Whenever the mood strikes, write a love letter to your mate, and express your heartfelt feelings or gratitude for a little thing he or she did. The key to this book is that when it's in the closet, or a special drawer, that means there's nothing new added, but when you add a letter, be sure to place it on your mate's nightstand. This is a beautiful way to make your partner's day (or night) by pouring your heart out and expressing your appreciation for each other. On each of your anniversaries, pull out your "love book," and reread all the entries for a special tradition that will mean a great deal throughout the years.

A Year To Remember ◎ If the couple enjoys fine wines, have a "restock the bar" party, and invite guests to bring something to update the couple's bar. A memorable twist on this would be to request that every guest search for a wine from a special year in their life: from when they were married, the years they had children, the year they purchased their first house, the year you met them, or any other year to remember.

Surprise, Surprise ◎ Joan Weiss, of Memphis, Tennessee, shared a particularly lovely anniversary surprise, one she arranged for two couples' twenty-fifth wedding anniversaries. She secretly invited their rabbi to renew the couples' vows, and went to great lengths to throw a second wedding for both pairs. She gave each of the couples a scrapbook with the invitation, cards, and photos of the evening. The wedding was a poolside party. They had a champagne fountain, and a cake made out of live flowers that made a beautiful centerpiece.

Write A "Why I Love You" Letter ◎ Every single year, make a promise to each other to write a "Why I Love You" letter, and on your anniversary eve, share the letters by reading them out loud. Store the letters in a special box, and read them throughout the year on Valentine's Day, and other times you want to share your feelings. This box of love letters will become a treasured memory for you, and for generations to come. As you write your letter, remember the little things, and be specific.

Etched In Time ◎ While a set of glasses might not sound particularly memorable, there's a fabulous way to add your personal touch, and transform them into an anniversary gift that will be appreciated for a long time. Locate a source that can etch drinking glasses, and have each glass etched with their names, and wedding date, and year. Or, if you want to give an entire set, include pairs of words to be etched on each glass that reflect your wishes and their love, such as "Phyllis and Jack, Love and Joy, Forever and Ever."

To Our VIP (Very Important Pair) ◎ Give the couple a pair of something, ranging from a pair of candlesticks with a colorful selection of candles, or matching bookends for two of a kind. Add a note that says, "Glad you two paired up!"

The Anniversary Cake ◎ Another anniversary memory that is still going strong centers around a cake that Sylvia Weinstock created for one couple. Since Sylvia created their wedding cake years ago, the couple decided that every five years they would have her re-create the top, and the first layer. To date, Sylvia has continued baking their cakes and, most recently their twenty-fifth anniversary cake. Their wedding cake has remained a time-honored tradition, and become a special memory to look forward to, as their five-year anniversary celebrations continue.

Rare Vintages ◎ For an important anniversary, collect a case of fine wines bottled in years that have meaning to the person, or couple, being honored: the year they met, got married, had their first child, bought their first house, etc. Make a wine list to go with your gift, and write down each important event the bottle commemorates: "1930 was an exceptional year because that was the year you were married."

How "Suite" It Is ◎ If you've never booked a gorgeous suite in a fabulous hotel, go ahead and splurge. Indulge your mate in total comfort, and have a romantic dinner for two. Then arrange for friends and family to appear for a special dessert and an anniversary surprise party you throw for your lovely bride of however many years. Toast her in front of all your loved ones, and pledge your love to her forever. When the clock strikes twelve, you both turn into pumpkins, and bid everyone farewell!

Faraway Wishes ◎ If a very special couple is having a big anniversary, and the family is spread throughout the country or in different cities, arrange to have a conference call. Check into services that provide these types of calls, and get family members from all over the country on the line, and let everyone say hello, read a special poem or offer best wishes, and make a huge fuss. These faraway wishes will hit home and be very memorable to everyone on the line.

The Anniversary Club ◎ A wonderful idea a group of our friends created is called "The Anniversary Club." Since they were all married during the same year, they have a yearly anniversary celebration, and go out to dinner together on their big day. One year they had a caterer prepare a special dinner. This yearly tradition has become a lovely way to celebrate their marriages, and get together with special friends as well.

Love adds a precious seeing to the eye.

—William Shakespeare

B
is for Birthdays To Remember

Happy Birthday! You've waited the entire year for this big day, and it should be really special. When it's your birthday, you get to be the center of attention. This is also what makes it quite a challenge for everyone involved. When someone's special birthday is near, the pressure is on. However, all you have to do to unlock some birthday magic is to consider your ultimate goal: the key to making a birthday memorable is to make him or her feel really special, since this is the day in history when they arrived in the world!

When a family member or friend does something really meaningful for me on my birthday, it reminds me how much one person can do to impact another's happiness. I try to do the same for others. For example, ahead of time, make sure the birthday boy or girl is covered that day. Don't leave her wondering if anyone will remember! Offer to take her to lunch or dinner. And, on the actual day, make sure their birthday begins with a wake-up call, card, or instant hug! You only have a few minutes to make that instant "initial" birthday impression, and it's memorable to be the first to call, or utter those words, "It's your birthday!"

The following suggestions will help you make someone else's birthday memorable. Select special ways to commemorate their special day.

A Jewel Of An Idea © Want to make a birthday gift really memorable? Add sentiment to your gift, and combine your birthday girl's birthstones with your birthstone, that of a loved one who is no longer present—to keep them close to her heart, or that of other special family members, and have them set together in a beautiful necklace, or piece of jewelry. From your birthstone combined with your significant others, to all of the grandchildren's birthstones for a grandmother, birthstones that have meaning, when set together, become even more memorable when they are combined into a beautiful bracelet or necklace. Here's a list of birthstones month by month:

Month	Color	Stone
January	Dark red	Garnet
February	Purple	Amethyst
March	Pale blue-green	Aquamarine
April	White (clear)	Diamond
May	Bright green	Emerald
June	Cream	Pearl or moonstone
July	Red	Ruby
August	Pale green	Peridot
September	Deep blue	Sapphire
October	Variegated	Opal or tourmaline
November	Yellow	Topaz or citrine
December	Sky blue	Turquoise or blue topaz

A Shopping Spree To Remember © Surprise a teenager, or anyone who loves to shop (or finds it difficult), with a shopping spree at a favorite store, or the mall. But this isn't any ordinary shopping spree and has some strings attached! Arrange ahead of time the assistance of a seasoned salesperson to treat her like a queen. Let her pick out a brand new outfit, accessories, and a fabulous pair of shoes to match, but with one condition: she has to leave the mall or store wearing the new outfit (or as much of it as possible, like the shoes, jacket, purse, etc.). Then, take her to a surprise birthday dinner, and have her best buddies waiting, or your entire family.

Music To His Ears © Well-known author, Gail Evans, did a memorable thing for her son's birthday. He lives in another city and loves to play guitar and sing, so Gail researched on-line voice coaches, and interviewed them by telephone long-distance, to find the best choice. Then, across the miles, she bought a gift certificate for lessons, and presented it to him on his special day. Her gift was music to his ears!

Zoo–ming In On A Special Birthday © When Arnold Weiss had a very special big birthday, his wife Joan surprised him with a family outing he'd remember forever. Joan rented a fifteen-passenger van and had everyone on board for a huge surprise. When he boarded, they all yelled "surprise," and then Joan drove him, their children, and grandchildren to the zoo, a favorite spot for all of them. When they got there, a professional video cameraman followed them throughout the entire zoo, and captured the entire day's outing. She even arranged with the zookeeper to let them all take turns climbing on a ladder to feed the giraffes. When they arrived at the gorilla's cage, there was an official from the zoo there to unveil a sign that said that they had adopted a gorilla named "Tumi" in honor of Arnold's birthday. (Note: Many zoos have a contribution program like this where you make a donation, and your name is posted, or an acknowledgment card is sent stating that you have adopted the animal.)

Queen For The Day © Nancy Joffre shared her favorite birthday present ever: "I woke up on my thirty-sixth birthday to our family tradition—breakfast in bed. My husband, Steve, woke the girls early, and they were so excited to make Mommy waffles, and orange juice. And, as is the tradition, everyone gets to eat in bed, not just the birthday person! I thought it couldn't get better, until my husband turned on his laptop computer to show me a slide show of all of us, with the background music playing our wedding song, "Have I Told You Lately That I Love You?" It was the most memorable birthday present, ever. That two-minute slide show had taken him hours to put together."

Strangers In The Night © For Betti Mori's husband's birthday, two (guy) friends of his went to a shopping mall with a video camera, several weeks in advance. They "interviewed" a variety of people, cluing them in before filming. For instance, two little old ladies were asked, "Are you here at the mall shopping for Christmas gifts?" to which they replied, "No, we are here to say Happy Birthday to Jean Mori." Everyone interviewed was a total stranger to the Moris and the "video guys." The videotape was played, and presented to Jean, at a surprise party with many friends. Other parts of the video consisted of interviews with his children, who presented a poem about their father, and a dance skit by four couples who were long-term friends. This was in addition to the mall interviews. It was a very creative gift, one that they still enjoy viewing fifteen years later!

My Most Precious Gifts ⓒ Whenever anyone asks me, what are the most precious gifts I've ever been given, naturally I think of my children. When they were born, I began a birthday book for each of them, and on the occasion of their birthdays, or a special event in their lives, I still write them letters reflecting their accomplishments, and my feelings about what wonderful individuals each of them have become. I also recorded funny things they said when they were little, and these have kept us rolling over the years. These "birthday" books continue to be ongoing gifts that I add thoughts to each year, and we enjoy reading the entries together as a family.

Show Me The Money ⓒ Here are some fun ways to give money, cash, bills, the works. Give the number of bills that reflect the age of the person, or frame a bill for a memorable gift:

- **$1.00**—George Washington, Great Seal of The United States (on the back). *You're the one I love, You're my one and only, I cannot tell a lie . . . I love you!*
- **$2.00**—Thomas Jefferson, The signing of the Declaration of Independence (on the back). *Congratulations on your new independence! Just the TWO of us, You're "TWO" Special* or, send lots of $2.00 bills and a note that says, *" 'TWO' our favorite son!"*
- **$5.00**—Abraham Lincoln, The Lincoln Memorial (on the back). *Give me five! Congratulations!*
- **$10.00**—Alexander Hamilton, U.S. Treasury Building (on the back). Create a top-ten list why you adore him or her.
- **$20.00**—Andrew Jackson. *I have 20/20 vision and only have eyes for you!*

Write A Birthday Letter ⓒ Inspired by a letter I once received via e-mail from a special friend on my birthday morning, I now try and do the same for other special birthday occasions. Here's an example of how to personalize your letter to express your wishes:

Dear _____,

You have made the world and my world so remarkably special, and I just wanted you to know this morning that you are indeed a gift to us all. I hold you close to my heart, and your happiness on this day and every day is supreme, and a priority to me. I know you will be reminded through many e-mails and telephone calls how many people love and cherish your entire being! You are simply a treasure to all of us who are lucky enough to call you a friend. With my deepest admiration, friendship, and love always, have a wonderful day and year ahead—you so deserve it! Happy Birthday _____!

Your devoted friend and fan for life, _____

Big Birthdays

Stretching Your Point ◎ For her thirtieth birthday celebration, one woman's husband showed up at her office in a limo filled with balloons and flowers, with her suitcase packed, and took her to an undisclosed location via airplane. He had arranged all the details with her boss, who was in on the surprise. Not until the cab driver pulled up in front of their hotel accommodations in the middle of Times Square in New York City did she know where they were going.

It's In The Bag ◎ Diane Smith shared a particularly special way her husband acknowledges her birthday every year. She said, "Since I begin celebrating my birthday days ahead of time, my husband puts out a little birthday bag, as we call it, and each day as my birthday approaches he puts little gifts in the bag every morning. The gifts are small with little notes, but this little tradition paves the way to my special day, and makes me really feel special and loved."

Love At Forty ◎ If your birthday girl or boy is a tennis player, and turning forty, then celebrate her love-forty birthday bash with a tennis theme. Fill a tennis ball can with forty pieces of candy, and a piece of jewelry tucked neatly inside. "Serve" up a fabulous dinner with forty friends, and ask each guest to bring a birthday wish, and a story about why they love your guest of honor. Create a book called Love–Forty, and include all the birthday expressions.

Garden Party ◎ Alice Hicks, who runs The Zodiac Room, the restaurant at Neiman Marcus in Atlanta, shared a memorable party. She wrote, "Probably the most memorable party was for a forty-fifth birthday. It was a garden party, in honor of a birthday girl who loved to garden. All the friends brought in potted plants, flowering plants, trees, etc. The room looked like a garden. The cake was fashioned after a huge watering can, with flowers, and the tables were covered with pastel green and pink cloths."

A Heartfelt Luncheon © On my friend Lorie's fiftieth birthday, a group of her friends got together and planned a beautiful luncheon at the private room in a special restaurant. The theme of the party was a take on the TV show *I Love Lucy*, but we changed it to *We Love Lorie*, and everyone was instructed to bring a poem or short story to add to a scrapbook. Between courses, we read entries from the book, including those that friends and family members had sent her from other cities, and then we asked her mother to share stories about the day Lorie was born. We served her a strawberry shortcake birthday cake that said, "We love you berry much," and had the table covered with candy for the sweetest friend on earth.

A Ride Down Memory Lane © Here's a birthday idea that my friend Patty had for her friend Mimi. A group of girls rented a limousine and brought champagne and chocolates on board. They picked up Mimi and took her for a tour down memory lane. They visited her elementary school, high school, the homes she grew up in and topped off the day with a festive lunch. For Mimi, it was a nostalgic day celebrating her youth and her friends.

Blast From The Past © Joan Weiss shared a special birthday surprise that one husband gave his wife. "A husband of one of my high school friends called six of his wife's friends from school to surprise her for all of our fiftieth birthdays. We had not seen each other since graduation. We all flew to her hometown and had the best time of our lives. Sixteen years later, we are getting together at least once a year. What a wonderful thing he did for all of us!"

For The Dad Who Has Everything © One Dad, who said he didn't want a thing for his sixty-fifth birthday, and then made sure everyone agreed to his wish, was overcome with joy when his family found a very creative way to commemorate his big day. His wife, their children, and his siblings joined together for a family group gift. They purchased a beautiful silver money clip and had it engraved with his initials. What then made it so memorable was that they put a check in it made out to his favorite charity for $650—$10 for every year! This meaningful donation in his honor was the ideal gift, and something he really valued.

Fiftieth Birthdays

Roses Are . . . Ready ◎ Forget a dozen roses, and go for an entire vineyard of wishes. You'll be remembered forever if you do what our friend Lyons did for his wife, Gail. He sent her a single rose stem on her fiftieth birthday with a note that said she would receive a rose every Monday for the next fifty weeks. Suggestions for following weeks include:

For the second week's note:	Just the two of us!
Third week	Three's a charm—for my charming wife.
Fourth week	Here's week number four—I couldn't love you any more.
Fifth week	Week number five—Thank goodness you're alive!
Sixth week	Here's to week number six—you're the only one I'd pick.
Seventh week	What to say for week number seven: When I'm with you I'm in heaven.

A Recipe For Friendship ◎ Create a recipe for a special person. Here's one I did for my friend Lorie:

Take 50 cups of Lorie.
Mix with a group of adoring friends and family.
Stir in a heaping birthday celebration.
Let it simmer and cool.
Slice it into memories for a lifetime.
Serve generously.

Eighty-five Wishes For An Eighty-fifth Birthday.

The Madson family had a particularly clever idea for their dad on his eighty-fifth birthday. His family got together and came up with eighty-five things to wish him, and created a list. They went around the room at his party, and everyone read the entries. This list showed great thought for his big birthday, and here are some of their prize-winning wishes:

1. May you live to be at least one hundred and many more!
2. May your teeth keep on working
3. May you win the "Octogenarian With The Most Hair" award
4. May your morning eggs always be just the way you like them
5. May your kids always remember to call
6. May the sun shine on your birthday
7. May the morning paper bring you good news
8. May your ship come in before your pier collapses!
9. May the joy you feel today be magnified
10. May you know with certainty that your children love you

. . . And the list went on, filled with seventy-five more memorable wishes!

Zodiac Signs © Want to give a memorable gift, but all you know about the person is the date of their birthday? Shoot for the moon, the stars, and the sun. Refer to popular magazines that list horoscopes, get a book on horoscopes, purchase something involving their zodiac sign, and create a gift that centers around their special qualities!

January 20 to February 18	Aquarius (the Water Bearer)
February 19 to March 20	Pisces (the Fish)
March 21 to April 19	Aries (the Ram)
April 20 to May 20	Taurus (the Bull)
May 21 to June 21	Gemini (the Twins)
June 22 to July 22	Cancer (the Crab)
July 23 to August 22	Leo (the Lion)
August 23 to September 22	Virgo (the Virgin)
September 23 to October 23	Libra (the Balance)
October 24 to November 21	Scorpio (the Scorpion)
November 22 to December 21	Sagittarius (the Archer)
December 22 to January 19	Capricorn (the Goat)

C

is for Christmas, Chanukah, and Kwanzaa

These holidays are eagerly anticipated all year long, so when they finally arrive, you certainly want them to be incredibly special. Holiday memories are what tie friends and family together and can be rich in tradition. From Christmas, to Chanukah, to Kwanzaa, the holidays are a time to celebrate traditions from the past, and create new memories to carry forward in years to come. Think of a memory created, or continued, as the best gift you can give anyone, especially your family, during the holidays. Those warm feelings when you're gathered around Grandma's famous chocolate cake at the dining room table with family and friends, or that memorable reminder of the smell of roasted turkey with all the trimmings—these add up to smiles on your family's faces, and what could be better?

The holidays, however, have become a time when so many of us are rushing and stressing over the little things, relentlessly searching for those perfect gifts, and checking those endless lists, that we forget treasured traditions, and get caught up in the hustle and bustle. Long after the gifts are unwrapped, it's still the traditions repeated year after year that ultimately stand out, and mean the most.

If you want to make this holiday season the best ever, don't side with Scrooge and stress over everything—plan ahead, and create new ways to make the holidays memorable and happy for everyone, including you! The following ideas are ways to make your holiday more memorable, and include some of the best ideas I've discovered.

Christmas

Homemade For The Holidays © Cara Lamb shared how her family goes to great lengths to create a memorable Christmas. She said, "Our family has a totally homemade Christmas and has done this for generations. Everyone spends the year working on creating his or her Christmas gifts by hand. Last year I made steppingstones with concrete and mosaics for everyone's gardens or backyards. One year my mother used our clothes from when we were babies and made them into quilts and throws, my aunt made soap, and my other aunt and uncle made me a piece of furniture—something they do every year in their workshop, and this time it was a beautiful spice rack. Another favorite gift was from a relative who took old windows and transformed them into gorgeous bed-and-breakfast trays. Another family member gives incredible framed photographs he shoots of landscapes. My aunt made my mother (her sister) a hand-painted chair, and on the bottom of the chair she attached a cherished photograph of the two of them when they were children. Every gift is filled with such love."

Seasons Greetings © Every year, one growing family poses in a familiar spot in their front hall, right by the stairwell, and has a family picture taken. Only, this is not an ordinary photo: each family member has to hold something they treasure, love to do, or are most proud of that year, and it's listed in the card by their name. One year, a family member became an author, and he was holding his book, his grandmother was holding her prized chocolate cake, and a teenager with a huge smile was dangling the keys to the car, since he had just gotten his driver's license. These photographs have become a time-honored tradition over the years, and are proudly displayed at Grandma's house, on what they call the Family Wall of Fame.

Just Fore You! © Stedman Graham recalled his best ever Christmas surprise: when Oprah Winfrey gave him a beautiful golf bag. What made the surprise so extra special, however, was how she presented it, and what was inside the bag. Stedman commented, "If anyone ever wants to give a great gift to a golfer, golf balls are the answer. A golfer loses golf balls all the time. On Christmas, Oprah surprised me with a golf bag filled to the brim with the best golf balls—and not just a few, but loads of them! I will never forget what a great gift that was, and I really put it to use!"

All In The Family Scrapbook © This is a wonderful gift that keeps on giving: a family I know purchases a scrapbook every year and keeps it at Grandma or Grandpa's house. When they visit, everyone adds new entries, photographs, and details. It gives the kids a fun activity to do while visiting; however, the book stays closed until Christmas. The eldest daughter explained, "The trick is to add things that really express your appreciation for each other—special sentiments, letters of thanks, artwork by the kids—capturing the year-long memories made, and then sharing them on Christmas at your family party."

Ornamentally Speaking © Start a tradition, and have an ornament party. Invite guests to bring an ornament based on a theme you dictate in your invitation (toys, musical instruments, fairy tales, the color white, etc.) to donate to a homeless shelter, or a family in need. Then take all the ornaments and package them up in a container that will carefully save them for years to come, and deliver them to a facility to help brighten the holidays for those less fortunate. Take a photograph of the tree each year and make that your thank-you note, or the invitation for the following year.

All Aboard For Christmas! © Pete Wilkerson's favorite holiday tradition is setting up the train his dad set up for him as a child. Pete commented, "Around our tree, we would set up the train the first of every December. I now carry that tradition on with my son, and it is fantastic when my dad comes down for the holidays, and we tell stories about when I was a little boy."

Ornaments Around The World © One of the nicest traditions I know of is one a mother had for her children that she now continues for her grandchildren: whenever she, or a close friend, travels, she brings back each grandchild a Christmas ornament. She then records in her Christmas Ornament Journal the date, where it was bought, and something special about the place the ornament came from—sharing its history or something of importance about the location. She also buys herself the same ornament and the weekend after Thanksgiving the entire family comes to her house for a family supper, and the children are presented their ornaments with the history of each one. They help Grandma decorate her tree with her new additions, and take home their set for decorating their own tree.

Food, Glorious Food © One of the nicest deeds you can do for someone is to find out what their favorite memorable food from their childhood was, do a little research, and then actually make it. If the individual who made it is alive, then see if you can get the recipe, or a lesson, and bake or make a great big batch. My radio co-host, Cindy, at Star 94, loves her grandmother's cooking. While discussing this particular food on-air, my co-host Ray researched it on-line and, within seconds, found out that it was a Russian dish. Cindy was thrilled to know the recipe actually existed, and now we know just what to make for Cindy to brighten her day! Only, we might have to call Grandma for some cooking tips.

Timeless Traditions © When you are first married, it may be difficult to continue every tradition from your combined families. Finding one meaningful family tradition to incorporate into your new lives together can make the holidays special. For example, every Christmas, a friend's husband received a nutcracker from his grandparents. The nutcrackers were dated at the bottom, and over the years he built up quite a collection. When it was time for their first Christmas together, his wife decided to continue the tradition, and give a nutcracker to her husband every year. The first year, she considered his love for *Star Wars*, and bought him a Darth Vader nutcracker and, to put a new twist on the tradition, she also started giving things with nutcrackers on them, not just the figures themselves—a nutcracker rug, a nutcracker ornament, etc. Each Christmas, he is excited to see what he'll get, and continues to build new memories based on cherished ones from the past.

Distinctive Decorations © Every year, have each family member purchase, or make, a special ornament recognizing a goal that he or she achieved that year, or something that is important to him or her. For example, if that year your child made all A's, the ornament could be collaged with copies of his report card. Or, if you took up tennis, the ornament might be a tennis ball with the year written on it. The more creative, the more memorable! Your tree will become a family museum of memories. Each person gets to put his ornaments on the tree, and talk about his accomplishments, and favorite ornament memories from years past.

International Christmas © Each year, pick a theme and celebrate part of Christmas learning about how other cultures celebrate this holiday around the world. For example, in Mexico on Christmas Day, a piñata, filled with trinkets, toys, and sweets, is hung from the ceiling for the children who, blindfolded, try to strike it with a long stick. In Holland, children clean their wooden shoes, stuff them with hay and carrots, and place them on the windowsills in their homes.

I'll Be Home For Christmas © For every special ornament you buy for your tree, buy duplicates for each child, and tuck them away in individual boxes. For the first Christmas your child is away from home, send him or her a box full of treasures that will make his or her tree as special as the one at home. Paige Janco's mother did this for her and it was the best gift of all.

A Key For Santa © A common question for children in houses and apartments without chimneys is, "How is Santa going to come in?" Many parents answer, "the windows," or even "it's magic," but this idea requires some mom-and-dad teamwork. Once your child begins to ask, present her with a special Santa Key. Have the child decorate the key, and tie a ribbon around it to hang on your doorknob, or on your door wreath.

Homemade For The Holidays © Decorate a jar, or tin, and fill it with homemade goodies. Send the jar to a member of your family, and start a tradition. The recipient has to modify the decorations and refill the jar to send to another family member. Keep this repeating, and everyone will be excited to see who gets the jar next. It can be great fun to log where the jar has traveled, especially if you live far apart from other family members. Be sure to include a recipe with each transfer, and keep all of the recipes with the jar. You not only start a fun family tradition, you have a record of great family recipes.

Christmas Cards And Jingle Journals © Christmas cards are a great tradition to start, and they'll help you keep up with everyone, but to make them memorable include a little "jingle journal" of what your family has been up to the past year with photocopied pictures, and information about each member.

Pur-r-r-fect Christmas © If you're a pet lover, then make sure to make your Christmas cards memorable. One suggestion is to take a photograph of your pet every year, and start a tradition of using that photograph on the front of the card. For a dog, add the greeting, "Bark . . . The Herald Angels Sing!" And for a cat use, "Have a pur-r-r-fectly wonderful Christmas," or "Here comes Santa Paws."

Singing Greetings © Change your answering machine message during the holidays to a jingle or carol that your entire family creates every year and sings together. For example, to the tune of "Jingle Bells," try this one: "Ring, ring, ring, Ring, ring ring, Ringing all the day, We're not home, but glad you phoned, and happy holidays!"

Chanukah

A Novel Idea © Have a book swap Chanukah party, and invite each guest to bring a favorite book they read this year. As guests arrive, cover each book with a colorful piece of Chanukah wrapping paper. Write on the package the age the book is suited for, and then swap books. Once everyone settles on the package they wish to open, they get to remove the wrapping paper to see what book they were given!

Chanukah Gathering © If your family is far away, and you must spend Chanukah apart, consider having a traditional yearly gathering of friends. Let your children invite a favorite friend and his or her family. Request that everyone brings a toy for a child who might not have one, and then donate the toys to a good cause. Create a theme for the evening, like games or books for the children to exchange. Put a price limit of five dollars on gifts, and have each person bring one to swap. Request that gifts be wrapped in clever ways to disguise what they are and, after lighting the Chanukah candles, exchange them until everyone decides which package they wish to open for keeps.

Musical Toys © Here's a fun group activity that kids will love at your classroom Chanukah party, or a gathering where there are a lot of kids. Ask that each child bring a wrapped toy with a value limit. Play musical toys—where the children sit in a circle and, when the music plays, pass the gifts around and around. When the music stops, the gift they are holding is the one they can keep. They can either get up and remove themselves from the circle, and open that toy, or stay in the game and keep passing until the music stops, and they get the package they desire. Since they have no clue what's in each package, some children will stay in the circle for a long, long time. Put a time limit on this activity, and watch the smiling faces, since there are no losers in this game!

And The Envelope, Please © Instead of bringing gifts for everyone, one family figured out how to stay on a budget, but still deal with their growing family, which was already huge. They spend only thirty-six dollars on gifts every year, and this has become the most popular gift idea of all time. Here's how it works: Each family takes eight envelopes, representing the eight nights of Chanukah, and puts the amount that corresponds to each night in a different envelope. For example, the first envelope is for the first night, and has one dollar. The second envelope is for the second night, with two dollars, and so forth until the eighth envelope has eight dollars. The envelopes are not marked, and every family puts their envelopes into a bowl, and they are mixed up. Each family member gets to choose one envelope. Everyone is given another turn until all of the envelopes are gone. This can also be done with just kids, and if you have a huge family you can add extra envelopes with single dollar bills in each to increase the odds for fun!

Chanukah "Make It And Bake It" Party © Throw a Chanukah baking party and bake up batches of fabulous recipes with friends and family. Ask everyone to bring their ingredients already mixed and ready to bake or make. Then spend the evening baking and making cookies, sweets, snack mixes, or anything else that's an incredible-edible, and fun to give as a gift. Once everything cools, let guests sample the goodies, and then fill containers to give as gifts to other friends and family members. Since Chanukah often begins earlier than Christmas, this is a nice thing to do for friends of different faiths. Have stickers, clever containers, and jars for wrapping up the goodies-on-the-go. It's the perfect way to wrap up Chanukah with a sweet memory.

Happy Challah–Days ◎ If you love to bake bread, or have a favorite source for challahs, the traditional bread served at Friday night dinners to welcome the Sabbath, then consider giving a challah (or a few for the freezer) with a note that says, "Happy Challah–Days!" Include freezing instructions and, to make your gift totally memorable, add a pretty challah cover, which can be found at synagogue gift shops or Judaica shops.

Collection Perfection ◎ A lovely time to start a collection for someone is during Chanukah. Help build it by giving a new addition every year. One grandmother gives her granddaughter beautiful kiddush cups (she brings them back from different cities all over the world), and gives them along with a check that says on it, "May your cup runneth over with happiness." The collection could be on any theme, though, that fits the individual's interests—from sports memorabilia, vintage toys, autographed books, to an object related to Chanukah, like a dreidel or a one-of-a-kind Tzedukah box (which can be found at synagogue gift shops and Judaica stores).

Kwanzaa

Fruits Of Kwanzaa ◎ Do a little homework, and learn all about the holiday customs and seven basic principles of Kwanzaa—which stand for unity, self-determination, collective work and responsibility, cooperative economics, purpose, creativity, and faith. Involve the entire family, and design art activities to do during Kwanzaa, and watch how the creative sparks will fly. Kwanzaa is also the festival of the harvest, so why not let the children learn to make some special foods from fruits and vegetables, and create a Kwanzaa cookbook?

The Festival Of The Harvest ◎ Since fruits and vegetables, the result of the harvest, are an integral part of the Kwanzaa celebration, give friends, teachers, and family members a basket generously filled with beautiful ripe mangoes, bananas, peaches, oranges, plantains, and other favorites. In the spirit of Kwanzaa, and the principle of Ujima, which means helping the community, focus on the fruits of your labors, and join together with another family and collaborate on a special project to benefit others. From bringing books to the library of a nearby children's hospital, to gathering fruit in season for a nearby homeless shelter, design a project that will help others.

Read All About It ⓒ There are several books that will help you to explain Kwanzaa to friends. For children, give *Let's Celebrate Kwanzaa*, by Helen Davis-Thompson. It's full of activities for kids three-to-ten years old. *Kwanzaa: Everything You Always Wanted to Know But Didn't Know Where to Ask,* by Cedric McClester, explains the seven basic principles of the holiday along with customs and suggestions.

The only gift is a portion of thyself.

—Henry David Thoreau

D

is for Dynamite Décor and Dazzling Centerpieces

O h, those outrageous centerpieces. You know, the kind that make a party special and everyone oooo and ahhh! Memorable décor and superior centerpieces welcome guests in a creative way, and add a great deal of pizzazz to a party or special celebration. Decorations set the tone of a function, adding ambiance, and an atmosphere. Since first impressions are the most memorable re-membrances, how can you create a memorable décor or centerpiece that will make your special occasion or event go down in party history?

My favorite centerpieces and décor are always unpredictable and over-the-top creative. To make your décor memorable, always consider whom the party is for and, if you are entertaining guests, pull out your favorite photographs of times shared, and create your centerpieces around those. A touch of sentiment works every time! Framed family photographs can help out in a pinch when you don't know what to use, or if you own a wonderful collection of glass paperweights in every color of the rainbow, or a doll collection, don't hesitate to pull out your prized possessions.

And last but not least, décor and centerpieces must be integrated into your overall theme with a focus, so check out the chapters on "Enticing Entertaining," "Parties With Panache," and "Fabulous Favors." Each of your finishing touches will make your occasion momentous if you select a theme and then carry it out with consistency.

Festive Centerpieces

An Evening In White Satin ◎ An unforgettable dinner table was decorated with white candles placed down the center of the table, and white china on crisp white tablecloths. The host had also tied white satin ribbons around the white napkins, and it was absolutely exquisite. What also made the décor so memorable was how it sparkled, and the table was pristine clean. She also took little strands of faux pearls and tied them around the wine glasses, and placed white orchids in little bud vases by each place setting. The hostess used splashes of color by carefully choosing seasonal fruits and vegetables that practically popped off the plates, since they were so eye-catching. To top off the evening, she served white chocolate mousse, covered with white chocolate shavings and bright red berries.

Legendary Tables ◎ Tony Conway of Legendary Events has been overseeing parties for many years, and suggests avoiding using one large floral centerpiece. He said, "When entertaining for a dinner party, instead of a big vase of flowers in the center of the table that no one can see over, use twenty-four single bud vases in the center of the table. If you have a long rectangular table, place them down the center, and mix them with triple the amount of votives with candles. Put the candles on unusual bases, like wine bottle coasters or completely flat picture frames, to accentuate them. Illuminate the table with candles of varying heights to make your setting just spectacular."

Cupcakes Gone Wild! ◎ Cupcakes are one of the most delicious and versatile ways to create a centerpiece or festive table. They can be stacked up on tiered cake plates, used as holders for place cards, or transformed decoratively. Cupcakes can also relate to any and every theme on earth, and all you have to do is ice them in your color scheme, or place flags or cupcake toppers (available at cake and craft stores) on top of each one. You can even ice up a cake to look like a giant cupcake by loading up the icing only on the top of the cake. Fun themes include, "Our cup–cake runneth over thanks to friends like you!" or "You take the cup–cake!"

Lazy Susan Centerpieces ◎ Denise Rindsberg of Let's Celebrate, a special-event decorating company, shared one of her most memorable center-pieces ever, one that her company did for a large event. "We designed thirty-inch lazy Susans for the center of each dining table. We then created a centerpiece that held loads of candy and a variety of snack foods. The centerpiece was placed in the middle of this design, which rotated each time guests wanted a choice of candy. Small scoops were supplied to help people help themselves to the different candies. This is also a clever idea for smaller-scaled centerpieces—you can layer up fresh fruit, snacks, or the food of your choice for a spinning center-piece that's functional, and highly creative.

Centerpiece Pizzazz ◎ Think out of the vase, and create a center-piece with pizzazz. For example, having a Texas-style barbecue? Fill western-style boots with fresh florals. Place a vase inside the shoe to avoid water spills and fill it with flowers or greenery. Want to be authentic? Select yellow roses from Texas! Or, how about filling high heels with pretty flowers for the theme, "No one can fill your shoes." Or, display a collection of something surprising—from antique toys, to a doll collection, to pretty glass paperweights—but get creative, and add the unexpected to make your table setting memorable.

Tea–riffic Centerpiece ◎ For a friend who has a teapot collection, we created a fabulous party featuring teapot centerpieces. Everyone who gave the party brought one of their own teapots, and we placed pretty flowers in each. The theme of the evening was "You suit us to a tea!" We all chipped in and got her a fabulous hand-crafted teapot for her collection, and ended the evening with—what else? Tea and color-ful teacakes! This idea is also a wonderful way to welcome a new member to the family, or someone to the neighborhood. If you prefer not to serve a meal, an afternoon tea also does the trick.

The Traveling Centerpiece ◎ One of the most memorable ideas one birthday group, who celebrated their birthdays yearly, had was to pur-chase a special centerpiece. It was a lovely silk topiary, in pink roses, that looked real. Whoever's birthday it was got to take the topiary home, and her job was to bring it back to the next person's birthday lunch as the centerpiece. Then that birthday girl took it home. The topiary tree has circled around six homes for over sixteen years and has become a time-honored tradition for a devoted group of friends.

The Center Of Attention ◎ Joni Alpert, a dedicated Habitat For Humanity volunteer, shared, "I recently attended a Habitat dinner with former President Jimmy Carter and his wife, Roslyn. The centerpiece was a large silver paint bucket filled to the brim with hydrangeas. Twenty-four-inch-long wooden rulers and metal tape measures were draped in the bucket, paintbrushes, and paint chip color samples, were in the centerpiece, and the color chips matched the lavender hue of the plentiful hydrangeas. The tablecloths were blueprints, and the napkin holder was a key ring tape measure. Paint samples were casually placed on the table on top of the blueprints to tie in to the whole theme. The best part was an American flag sticker was placed on the back of one of the evening programs, and the person who had that one got to take home the centerpiece. My daughter, Jaime, won the centerpiece, and we brought it home from the dinner, and I brought it into the Consumer Action Center to put on display for all of the volunteers to enjoy. I kept it fresh for quite a while by replacing the hydrangeas with ones from my garden."

Game Parties ◎ How about hosting a game party and creating a cake that looks like the game board to use as the centerpiece? Carry out the entire theme from start to finish. Invite guests to come over for "MONOPOLY and Meatloaf," or "Pictionary and Pizza." Make it a tradition that if you win the game, you get to host the next month's party.

Centerpieces For Children's Parties

Dip–pity Doodah ◎ Transform a dip into a delicious centerpiece and clever creation: Hollow out a large mound of bread and fill it with the dip of your choice, or egg or tuna salad. Using toothpicks, add smaller rolls and olive eyes, and create a monster for a festive way to serve your partygoers.

A Candy Centerpiece ◎ It's simple to make, but has a fabulous appeal to kids. Secure a cone-shaped large Styrofoam form into a clay or plastic weighted flowerpot. Add a decorative ribbon around the pot, and then begin, in an organized fashion, arranging the lollipops (or candy of your choice) around the form by sticking them into the form one line of pops at a time. You can alternate colors, or mix them up, for a rainbow of candy.

Bright Lights And Neon Designs ⊚ Neon centerpieces are always fun as they add a special glow to a party that has the lights dimmed. You can add a neon touch by using neon paints, or a variety of products that glow in the dark, including earrings, sticks, necklaces, and more. Check your local party store for "glowing" options.

Toy–riffic Centerpieces ⊚ Toys are fabulous holders for flowers, candy, and even food. They also make fabulous centerpieces when they fit the theme. Since they are often inexpensive, they add color and fun to a party or special occasion. For example, use game boards elevated on stands to hold the flowers or food presentations for a creative touch. Fill trucks, or a shiny red wagon (lined of course), with food for an added flair. Dolls of all shapes and sizes work well for a luncheon for living dolls, and plastic footballs can be cut and split to hold rolled napkins in the team's colors, and they can also be piled up on one another to create a football-fantasy display. Check out your toy closet if you have kids, and you just might find that your centerpiece is right under your nose.

Double-Stuffed Balloons ⊚ A secret of party planners who use balloons is to put a balloon inside a balloon for a special effect. Using clear balloons adds a special touch of elegance, and they can be mixed with flowers for a fun, but elegant look.

Play The Field ⊚ Transform your table into a fabulous setting for a sports-themed party by covering the table with inexpensive green AstroTurf. Put actual stadium cushions in each chair, and decorate the playing field with details that make it look real. Include a cake that is in the shape of a football as your centerpiece, raised up on a cake stand, and search for football-themed paper plates and napkins to add a festive touch. Small colorful footballs can be the place cards, and write each team member's name on theirs. Slice them open, and fill with chocolate footballs for a fun party favor.

Holidays

Pineapple Turkey ◎ Every Thanksgiving one of my favorite center-pieces is a pineapple, washed and dried and placed on its side, lying down in the center of a silver tray that is covered with lettuce. The leaves on the pineapple become the turkey's tail, and the opposite end will be transformed into its head. Select a squash that has a long neck, and connect it with toothpicks at the base of the pineapple, sticking upwards, to create the head and neck of the turkey. Then add eyes and the turkey's waddle, with red peppers cut for the waddle, and eyes from small sliced carrots. Take carnations, and colorful fall flowers, and line the base of the pineapple, or fill the tail, whichever you prefer, to create a sensational turkey that will be totally memorable.

Ahead Of The Holidays ◎ Here's a clever idea one couple does every fall for their friends. They get in the holiday spirit by wrapping up boxes in colorful Christmas and Chanukah wrapping paper. They then tape-wrap peppermint sticks around cans, and tie them in place with a ribbon, and fill the cans with water, and flowers. The candy-cane vases and wrapped gifts create a colorful centerpiece for what they call their "ahead-of-the-holiday party." Their tradition is to grill everyone on what they really want for Christmas or Chanukah.

Fruitful Centerpiece ◎ Pierce an orange with a floral tube that holds a stem and water. These are available at your local florist and used to keep the stems of cut flowers fresh prior to putting them in a vase. For a quick and colorful centerpiece add a few flowers cut a few inches under the bloom and insert them into the water-filled tube. Line the center of the table with these fruitful displays or place one at each individual setting.

E

is for Enticing Entertaining
and Incredible Edibles

Some people have a knack for entertaining, but for others it's a major undertaking. The key to successful entertaining is to have fun, but the secret ingredient is always to have plenty of fabulous food, glorious food, displayed with creativity, and mix the guest list with new friends, and old. As the host or hostess, if you are enjoying yourself during the party, it's more likely your guests will, too. Entertaining with pizzazz is also a way to give others a gift of memories shared, fabulous food, and the special camaraderie of being together. So what is my goal when I entertain? I think of how to make my guests feel especially at home and totally comfortable. And with that said, I make every effort to do as much as possible ahead of time so that I can enjoy the evening as well.

The other secret of talented entertainers is to always consider your guest's tastes, their likes and dislikes. Appeal to all of their senses for a sensational evening, and mix up people who don't all know one another. Adding your signature style is what it's all about, and giving everyone who attends a memory to enjoy.

Top Tips For Making It Memorable

- Select a theme. Even if you throw a dinner party, adding a theme adds pizzazz! Carry out that theme in your color scheme and centerpieces, and serve it up with style!

- The secret to a great party is to mix your guests, so that they have two degrees of separation in common. Put people together with common interests as well as diverse backgrounds—but put them at ease by introducing them and stating what they have in common to get the conversations rolling.

- Consider your guest's likes and dislikes. Are they health-food fanatics, gastronomy lovers, or even a mix of both? Get the lowdown on everyone's preferences, if possible, and plan your menu accordingly.

- Then remember the "Four P's": plan, prepare, and present it with pizzazz. Prepare everything you can ahead of time so that you can enjoy your guests.

Dinner Parties

Invite A Best Friend's Friend For Dinner © Invite two couples to dinner, and ask them to each bring a special couple they adore that you do not know. I call this party a "friend of a friend's party." Everyone ends up meeting someone new, and it's a wonderful and totally memorable way to create a lively dinner party, and meet your friend's friends and get to know them.

Dinner Party For A Few Good Eggs © One of our favorite dinner parties that our friends Larry and Patty give is their annual Omelette Party. Patty hires a chef who prepares made-to-order omelettes (yes, egg white, regular, with or without cheese . . . you name it!). She prepares all the ingredients ahead of time and puts them out in pretty bowls. Then she has a chef arrive for a few hours to do all the cooking and cleanup, so she can enjoy her company. Your dinner is made to order, and the side dishes are overflowing with hash browns, fresh fruit, and, later, indulgent desserts.

An Evening Of "Vine" Dining ⊚ Anything from the vine is the theme of the evening, from a tomato salad with grape tomatoes, to a divine tomato sauce and pasta, to the fruit of the vine and fine wines.

Menu Magic ⊚ A customized menu is a special way to enhance your dinner party or event. Easily created on a computer, or by hand, and then duplicated, a menu can carry out a special theme, and highlight the guest of honor, or theme of your party.

Thank The Cook Party ⊚ This idea prevails as one of the nicest things you can do for a family member who is always doing the cooking. Have a "thank the cook" party and insist on doing all the cooking. Present your "Best Chef" awards, written on paper plates, describing the dish, and why you love it (and them). Make sure your guest of honor doesn't lift a hand, and present a cake at the end of dinner that says on the icing, "Hail To The Chef!"

It's A Sandwich Party! ⊚ If children are coming to dinner, have a variety of sandwich meats and breads and challenge them to make a silly sandwich. Piled high, they are bound to layer it up with sandwich meats, bread, condiments, slaw, peanut butter and jelly, sliced bananas, and more! Also, have cookie cutters on the table so the kids can stamp their sandwiches into fun shapes. You could also have the kids make a long sub sandwich for extra fun. Serve ice cream sandwiches for dessert, or make your own with cookies and put ice cream in the middle.

Very Happy Meals ⊚ Invite a group of friends to a luncheon at your home, and serve the lunch in restaurant-style take-out boxes with your family name on them. For example, create a label on the computer, or write in big letters, (your name, i.e., "The Spizman's Eatery"). Include sandwiches, fruit, cookies all tied up with pretty bows, and little prizes just like they do at the fast food restaurants. Or, serve up each course in Chinese take-out boxes for a memorable presentation.

The Game of Life ⊚ Invite friends and family over for a special game night. Clear tables and set up stacks of great games that can be played in groups. If you have a large number, place names in a hat and draw groups for first games. Each group can pick a game from the stack and take it to their designated table. Redraw names after each round to mix up players. Find a game that the whole group can play together for the final round of the evening. This tradition can create fun rivalries that build excitement leading up to the big event, and it's fun to do it the same time every year.

Heart Of Gold Party © Perhaps you have a friend or family member who has done a great deal of nonprofit work, and you wish to honor him. Invite guests to pay tribute to his or her heart of gold. Make the theme of the evening "everything gold" and cover the table with lots of chocolate hearts of gold wrapped in gold foil. Wrap napkins in gold ribbon, use gold place mats, gold-colored china, or heavy paper plates, and everything you can find that celebrates his heart of gold.

One Big Happy Family © Invite your friends and their children to a Sunday evening get-together and have a picture-perfect party. Ask each guest to bring their favorite baby picture of themselves and, when the guests arrive, scramble the photographs and display them on a bulletin board, or a designated table. See who can match up the right pictures and create one big happy family.

A Hot Diggity Dog Party © From low fat, to the real deal, to chicken dogs, veggie, or soy dogs, and more, have a hot dog roast, and tons of toppings from chile, slaw, onions, relish, shredded cheese, sauerkraut, to mustard and ketchup. You can also have corn dogs and serve cookies and brownies in the shape of dog bones.

Carbo-Loading Party © This dinner party is ideal before the big race. Serve pasta and an evening of carbohydrates for those runners who love to stock up. Even your dessert bar can be filled with cheesecakes and fresh fruit. Add a sign to the buffet where you serve the food that says, "Carbo-loading Begins Here."

Creative Platters © Instead of serving food on platters, use records, Frisbees, and other really neat objects that lend themselves to tray-like surfaces. You'll make a clever statement and have everyone talking!

Perfect Place Cards

Tony Conway of Legendary Events shares his most memorable place-card settings:

- Edible Place Cards. Take a beautiful pear, orange, or apple and carve each guest's name into the pear using a special paring knife. Cut only the skin, and not into the fruit, to add a special touch. Or, try a vegetable like a fresh, clean artichoke, and place the name card between the leaves.

- Think Chocolate! Purchase chunks of chocolate and either stick the place cards into them with a place card holder or toothpick, or carve the name into the chocolate. Give everyone a bag to wrap up their place card and take it home with them after the party.

- Use a pretty flowerpot filled with flowers to hold the place card, or write the name on the pot in a pretty calligraphy. Also consider using an herb like basil, and on one side put the directions for caring for it, and on the other side put the guest's name.

Place Card Poems © One of my personal favorite place card creations was done for a special family event. To everyone's astonishment, I wrote an individual poem for every guest attending the party, and then printed them out on clear labels on the computer in a pretty script font. I then placed each label on a clear acrylic frame that was 3" × 4". Guests were so touched by their place card poems. This idea takes endless hours of time and is not recommended for anyone who doesn't like a challenge! Here's an example of one:

> *Mr. And Mrs. Doug Freedman*
> *Table Number* _____
>
> *As a sister and brother, you pass the test,*
> *We think you are the very best!*
> *No matter when, no matter where,*
> *We're happy you are always there!*

Cookie Place Cards © Edible place cards add a special touch when you have each guest's name written on a cookie so that the entire thing is edible. Cookies are very versatile and can be made in almost any shape and theme. From pocketbook cookies with each guest's initials, to T-shirt cookies with the guest's name on one side and their table number on the opposite side, a personalized cookie wrapped in a clear cellophane bag tied with ribbons makes a memorable place card that can be gobbled up after the party is over.

All On Deck ◎ Place cards can be really fabulous when you use something unique for the card. Type a guest's name and table on a sticker and place it on a card from a deck of cards. This is a colorful place card for a casino party, or for someone who loves to play cards, or someone who was dealt a great hand in life!

Name The Tables ◎ Instead of using numbers for your tables, name each table with a creative flair that matches the party's theme. For example, if you're having a party with a seated dinner and place cards, name each table after one of the birthday boy or girl's favorite hobbies, favorite baseball player, or store to shop at.

First Place Place Cards ◎ If you just finished a renovation, paint chips from your local paint store make clever place cards, or use squares cut from your old blueprint plans mounted on card stock. For a doctor, choose a mocked-up prescription for a happy evening. The wife of a golfer we know used golf tees sitting in tiny clay pots filled with Styrofoam, and with a permanent marker she wrote each guest's name on a golf ball that rested on the tee. Anything goes when it comes to place cards, and the more creative the better.

Incredible Edibles And Memorable Cakes

The Cake Master ◎ Sylvia Weinstock, the internationally known cake designer and baker in New York, shared her inside tips for making an event really memorable, and how a cake can serve as the centerpiece, or create a memory that complements an occasion. She commented, "What makes any event really memorable is your relationships with the guests, with the host, or a benefactor." The key is how you respond to your guests and make them feel welcome. Since Sylvia has created thousands of cakes for some of the most famous people in the world, I asked her what makes the most memorable cake memories, and she shared some helpful tips:

Make the cake a surprise. One of Sylvia's most memorable cakes was a large gold vase that was filled with flowers. What made it so memorable was that it mimicked to perfection other enormous vases that exquisitely adorned the ballroom. Each vase was centered under an arch and appeared to be part of the décor. When it came time to cut the cake, everyone wondered where the cake was, but imagine the surprised look on their "vases" when the centerpiece was sliced and served!

Make the cake's theme very creative. For example, Sylvia created an African safari cake covered with animals for a couple going on a safari. Another cake for the owners of a vineyard was a case of wine made from cake, and the labels on the wine bottles were photographs of the bride and the groom. For Donald Trump's wedding, she created an enormous cake that they had to build using a stepladder because it was so tall—it served over a thousand guests. She also created a golf bag cake for the retired president of the Masters Tournament that was the exact color of his bag, with his tees, clubs, keys, and golf towel. From Alice in Wonderland cakes with all the characters, to Simpson-figured wedding cakes, anything is possible!

Cupcake Cake © This is easy and fun to do, especially if you own stacking china or glass cake plates that are graduated in size. Begin by stacking the cake plates, and then fill each layer with cupcakes. For a baby shower for a girl, you could use all pink cupcakes, and use blue for a boy. Or, if they don't know what sex the baby is, combine both. Cupcake cakes make a festive presentation and are so pretty.

Iced To Perfection © Let the kids ice up with white icing a store-bought or home-baked cake after it cools. Then instruct the kids to cover the entire cake with a fun, creative design of M&M's, jelly beans, sprinkles, and bits and pieces of other candies. This cake will be one of their all-time favorites and so much fun to eat.

You Take The Cake! © According to Ryan McEntyre, who is from a family of over four generations of bakers in Atlanta, "One of our most popular cakes for little girls' birthday parties is the slumber party cake. We create a regular-shaped sheet cake, and transform the top of it with chocolate icing, and create a design of four or five sleeping bags in a row. Popping out of the tops of the sleeping bags are the children's heads peeping out. It's a huge hit every time." Other cakes that McEntyre's Bakery suggests you create include a cake in the shape of a driver's license, a telephone or cell phone with their telephone number on it, a replica of a pocketbook, a birdhouse (for bird watchers), or a running shoe for an athlete.

Chocolate Dipping Bar © In fondue pots, heat up the dipping chocolate (both milk, dark, and white chocolate) and have a party where everyone makes their own dipped indulgences. Have bowls of pretzel sticks, strawberries, apricots, cookies, and just about anything that would be delicious covered in chocolate, and have toppings that are fun to add like colorful sprinkles, chopped nuts, and more.

Martini Masterpieces © Serve foods in unusual containers, like martini glasses. From three different sorbets, to mashed potatoes, anything goes that's not too hot and is easy to eat. And think out of the glass here, because everything from macaroni and cheese, to a chicken salad in a pretty puffed pastry works. Or how about an ice cream-tini bar? That's what Legendary Events served at another party. They created a chocolate martini bar, and you filled a martini glass with ice cream, toppings of chocolate sprinkles, shavings, and white chocolate toppings.

Ice Carvings © Another artistic suggestion is to serve three scoops of different-colored sorbets in a beautiful ice carving. While this requires expert assistance, it's a gorgeous addition to make a meal memorable. And if you want to outdo yourself, have an actual ice carver carving an ice sculpture while dessert is being served.

Choo-Choo Cake © When I was a little girl, my mother had a cake made that resembled a train. She had six individual cakes in succession on a long cardboard platter that were iced and looked like a circus train. They had pretzel bars on the sides of each car and included clowns, animals, and colorful icing. The train was placed down the entire center of the table, and was the hit of the party, and a memory I'll forever cherish. All aboard!

An Edible Toast ◎ We were recently taken to dinner by special friends and, while at dinner, our friend Abby wished to toast our friendship. Since no one was drinking wine, he lifted an onion ring, one of which we had all just helped ourselves to, and asked us to raise our "rings" and join in the toast. As silly as it sounds, who says a toast can't be fried, tried, and devoured?! It certainly was memorable and gave us all a great laugh.

The Doughnut Cake ◎ Take doughnuts and layer them up as you would a layer cake, and use cake pedestals to separate the layers like you would with a wedding cake to add height. The layers can be iced with white icing, and you can add pretty iced flowers (or silk ones) all over the cake for an added touch.

State Of The Cake! ◎ Betti Mori's friend told her of a memorable cake she baked for the birthday party of a woman from New Jersey. She sketched out a map of New Jersey, enlarged it, and used it as a template. The layers were pieced together and cut to be a map of the birthday girl's home state. Two layers were stacked on a very large cookie sheet, with lemon curd between layers, and frosting on top. The hometown of the honoree was marked with a candle. Talk about a cake state-ment!

Clothesline Cake ◎ Sarah Cocroft shared her most memorable cake memory: "It was a birthday cake that my mom gave me when I was little. It had white frosting and a colorful clothesline that ran across the top of it with hanging doll clothing made of candy. It was so cute and original that I'll never, ever forget it."

Candy Sushi ◎ Here's an idea one mom shared that her kids adored: Using icing, small bits and pieces of gummy candy, shavings, and other items, let kids unwind fruit roll ups and minimally decorate the surfaces. Begin by spreading white icing on the flattened fruit with popsicle sticks and then placing a bit of colorful candy to mimic real-life sushi. Roll the fruit roll back up so that it's tightly wound, and then have an adult cut the sushi look-alike roll into pieces, just like the real thing. Serve with chopsticks for an added fun effect. The candy sushi will be a huge hit that's equally as much fun to make as eat.

Words To Add When Giving Edible Gifts

Candy

How sweet it is!

To the sweetest friend on earth.

Go-Diva!

Sweets for my sweets.

Sugar for my sugar.

Confectionately yours.

Confection perfection.

You're a lifesaver.

Candy is dandy and so are you.

Nothing is as sweet as you.

Pop-ping in to wish you a happy holiday.

Thanks for sticking with me!

Thanks for helping me out in a crunch.

Congratulations on your home sweet home.

I'd chews you as my friend any day!

Sorry I was so sour.

Cakes and Pies

You take the cake!

Working with you is a piece of cake.

To an angel (cake) of a friend.

Thanks for making my job easy as pie!

Any way you slice it, you're the best!

Have your cake and eat it, too!

You're the icing on the cake!

Life is short, eat the icing first.

Let there be cake!

A tisket a tasket, goodies are in this basket!

Other Edible Gifts

Coffee: I love you a-latte.

Thanks a-latte.

Tea: You're Tea-riffic.

You suit me to a tea!

Fondue: I'm fond-ue of you.

F

is for Fabulous Favors

The most memorable parties on earth have a fabulous favor for the guests to take home as a reminder of the party. But really memorable favors are kept for a long time and become happy reminders of the festive occasion. A great favor is also a surprise, which becomes a thank-you for attending the party. And who doesn't like a gift? We all do, and fabulous party favors are favored remembrances of happy times, and fond memories.

When selecting a favor, regardless of the occasion, think of something really useful or meaningful. Who wants another dust collector? Not me! So consider what type of favor is the best for bidding your party guests a special farewell. Favors are more memorable when you select something that celebrates and supports the theme of a party. And if the party is for someone special, the favor should relate in some way to the individual the party is for. That's what makes it really special and unforgettable.

The ideas presented below are favors that have been selected as some of the most memorable ever. They are not just reminders of a fabulous party, but an object or something a guest really appreciates being given.

Anniversary Party Favors

"Two" Clever! © When you can't think of favors to give out, consider giving two-dollar bills. That's what Joan Weiss does when she wants to be especially memorable. Instead of buying favors, she saves the time and extra effort and makes the money the favor. But not just any money—she locates two-dollar bills, which are still in print today. At first no one believes they are real, but that's one very real favor that won't be left behind. It's also a fun idea to give them out after a special couple's big anniversary party. The bill can be fan-folded or placed in a colorful envelope, and add a note that says, "Thanks *Two* You For Coming To _____'s Anniversary Celebration!" or "Happy Anniversary To Two Of A Kind!"

Smart Cookie © An edible party favor was created for a 50s-themed anniversary party a couple gave for their fiftieth wedding anniversary. It was a cookie that had their photo image on it. What made it so special, though, was that each cookie was in a special box on a table that said, "Goodnight Gracie," that held coffee and the cookies for the guests as they departed.

Birthday Party Favors

Shoestring Surprise © Tie a brightly colored shoestring or ribbon to a small toy, and place it in a colorful box or basket. The string should be about eighteen inches in length and tied in a knot on the opposite end. Let the strings hang outside the bag so that each child leaving the party can pull a string and get a surprise favor.

Candy Necklaces © Have a Hawaiian luau, but serve candy and loads of fun foods. Then, transform a Hawaiian lei into a candy necklace—it will be a huge hit with kids as they create it and craft with candy. Instruct children to take a Hawaiian lei necklace and fill it with candy to take home as a favor. Candy can be glue-gunned by adults if you want to make them for the kids or, if children are creating them, they can use pipe cleaners, or clear tape. From wrapped bubblegum to tootsie rolls and more, the goal is to attach wrapped candy to the entire lei to make a colorful candy necklace. Purchase the leis in a variety of bright tropical colors, and have an assortment of candy on hand.

The Best Medicine For Aging © Pill bottles are fun favors to use for adult birthday parties, especially for those celebrants who are over-the-hill. Fill the bottle with brightly colored M&M's and add a personalized label created on your computer that says, "Getting over-the-hill? Take one of these pills!"

What's In A Name? © Here's a favor that is a terrific activity to create at a party. At your local craft store, purchase wooden letters that are the first letter of each guest's name. Add a hanger to the back of each one so they can be hung on the wall. Cover the tables with a tablecloth, and place each wooden letter in front of a chair. Fill bowls on the tables with craft supplies, such as glue, stickers, magazine cut-outs, alphabet letters, odds and ends, and anything else you can use to collage and transform the letters. You could also use non-toxic washable paint, if you prefer, and guests could paint their letters. When all your guests arrive, instruct them to sit in front of the first letter of their name and begin decorating it. The letters can dry while you are eating cake (which is, by the way, in the shape of the birthday girl's name or initial), and then be taken home as a fabulous party favor.

Bookmarks © At a friend's birthday party, her sister-in-law stood up, and gave a tribute, and presented everyone with a bookmark created from a collage of photographs she had done. Each bookmark was laminated, and had a photo of the birthday girl that included her friends attending the party.

A Blast From The Past © Do a little research, and find out something that was invented the year the birthday boy or girl was born, and discover a world of fabulous favors. For example, in 1930, one of the most popular products known to man was invented—Scotch tape. This would be a fun item to hand out with a note—taped, of course, to the favor—that says, "Thanks for sticking with Jack on the occasion of his birthday!" In the 1930's, the game MONOPOLY was invented, so handing out dollar bills would definitely be memorable.

1900s—Crayons, Model T, tea bags

1910s—Crossword puzzles, LifeSavers, mechanical pencil

1920s—Bubblegum, yo-yo, masking tape, Band-Aid, Kool-Aid, Q-tips

1930s—Scotch tape, stereo records, the game Monopoly, ballpoint pens, chocolate chips

1940s—Color television, Silly Putty, mobile phone, Frisbee, jukebox, cake mix, Velcro, Scrabble, Slinky

1950s—First credit card, Mr. Potato Head, first diet soft drink, birth of McDonald's, Hula Hoop, Barbie doll

Baby Shower Favors

Oh Baby! © Fill little clear plastic baby bottles with candy-coated almonds, chocolate candy, or anything sweet. Tie pink or blue ribbons (or yellow if you don't know which sex the baby is) around the neck of the bottle for an adorable favor. To make this time-tested favor more memorable, add a strip of paper into the bottle with the baby's name, birth date, and weight and length.

Baby Sock Flowers © Take a baby sock in pink or blue and attach a wire stem to make each sock look like a rosette. Add some floral leaves for a baby sock rose. These are also adorable on top of rolled diapers that are held together by diaper pins to make a baby diaper cake. Cover it with baby toys, rattles, and odds and ends, plus bows for a special centerpiece.

Shower Your Guests © They came to the baby shower, so now shower them with something for the shower—from bath gels, to body lotions, or bubble bath. Guests will appreciate your thoughtful shower favor and put it to good use. You could also add a special sticker to a bar of soap that says the baby's name, birth date, and statistics.

Shower Your Guests With Love © Even though the baby shower was for you, bring gifts for all the hostesses that gave you the party. Buy small umbrellas, the kind you can tuck in a purse, and attach a note, "Showering you with endless thanks!"

Promises, Promises © Make a coupon booklet for each guest, entitling him or her to a bevy of baby kisses, honey-dipped hugs, gorgeous gurgles and, of course, one free diaper-changing opportunity.

Photo Op © Give each guest a pretty picture frame, with a note in the frame saying, "Coming Attraction: Watch this space for the starring attraction, coming soon." Be sure to follow up with a photo when the baby's born.

Wedding Favors

Lollipop Bouquets © Brides will love having a special bouquet for their wedding rehearsal practice, or as a favor for the bridesmaids to take home from a shower. Purchase a Styrofoam bouquet form, which usually holds flowers, at a craft store. Instead of live flowers, insert Tootsie Roll Pops to cover the top. In place of a floral bouquet, the lollipop bouquet adds a sweet touch to a special day, and sets the style for the sweetest bride on earth.

Breakfast To Go © When one couple's wedding ended in the wee hours of the morning, they gave out to all parting guests a breakfast baggie filled with two bagels, cream cheese, and jars of assorted jellies. The note enclosed said, "Breakfast to go—Love Sally & Joe."

Sweet Dreams © Fill a plastic champagne glass with sweets, and wrap it up in white tulle with pretty white ribbons. Add a note to the favor that says, "Sweet dreams from _____."

A Swanky Hanky © As guests arrive at a wedding, give out handkerchiefs with a quote about love written in fabric paint (or embroidered for a smaller wedding). This will take some time, but will definitely make a statement. Trim the handkerchief with the colors of the wedding for an added touch of pizzazz. See "Q is for Quotes" for words of love to choose from.

A Recipe For Love © When Seth and Wendy Goldberg got married, they decided to create the ultimate wedding favor and keepsake. Together they combined efforts to compile a cookbook of their family's favorite recipes. Ahead of time, each guest was asked to send a famous recipe from their family's table. From Grandma Fran in New Orleans to Grandma Edna on the Lower East Side of Manhattan, and from Etoufe (Wendy's Favorite) to Potato Latkes (Seth's favorite), everyone's specialties were included. Wendy did some research and located a company that published cookbooks, but you could compile one and simply have it printed and bound at a quick-copy store. Wendy and Seth still get calls throughout the year from family and friends expressing their thanks for the wonderful recipes they received as a reminder of a memorable wedding and a very special couple. Word is they are planning a 10th Anniversary edition!

Bar Mitzvah Favors

A Book To Remember © While many of the favors mentioned above will work for Bar and Bat Mitzvah parties, a memorable favor that everyone admired was presented at each place setting at Adam Brown's Bar Mitzvah. It was a small four-by-five-inch book created by Adam's parents, with his name in large letters on the cover, and a place for the guest's name, and table seating. As you opened the book, there was a photograph of Adam and a letter from him thanking everyone for helping him reach this special day. Then came a poem: "From north to east to south to west, We are delighted to have you as our guests!" Listed were all the cities that out-of-town guests came from and a thank-you to the family and friends who entertained. The memorable addition to the booklet was a letter from Adam's grandfather that read:

My Dearest Grandson Adam,

On this wonderful occasion, it gives me a great feeling to see my only grandson become a Bar Mitzvah. I have seen you as a beautiful child taking your first steps, and now have the pleasure of seeing you take your next step into manhood. Yes, Adam, you are starting on a journey into life, and each step you take can be very rewarding as long as you take the path of righteousness and unselfishness, loving God, and family. Staying on this path throughout life can only bring fulfillment and happiness for you and your loved ones. Thanks again for being that grandson I've always dreamed of having.

With all my love,
Grandpa Ben

G

is for Graduation Celebrations and Gifts

I s someone special graduating from middle school, high school, or college? A religious program or a master's program? Or how about law or medical school? If so, then you've turned to the right place. Graduation is a special time and calls for a special celebration. Graduates usually want one thing, and it's very green. You got it! Money of any denomination will do. The key, though, is to give it in a creative fashion—so clever, in fact, they actually remember it long after it has been spent. Grads always have a wish list of things they want as they embark on the next step in their careers. Their wants range from gadgets, laptops, cell phones, televisions, and whatever is in vogue in the electronics world.

As you celebrate your graduate's accomplishments or give a graduate a gift, consider ways to make it totally memorable, from the gift-wrap to the friends and family who attend. Even though they might appear too cool for a fuss, they'll love every second of it.

Graduation Celebrations

Certificate of Appreciation ◎ When our son Justin graduated from college, he gave each family member a certificate of appreciation. On the computer, he created a diploma of recognition for our support, dedication, and the love that we had shown him through the years, and had each one laminated at a quick-copy store. It was the perfect ending to the perfect weekend, and a memento each one of us treasured.

A Tea–riffic Celebration ◎ High tea—high hopes! Here's a lovely way to bid farewell to your daughter's girlfriends as each girl goes in a different direction. Invite your daughter's friends and their mothers to join you and your daughter for tea. A buffet of finger sandwiches and scones will complement the party and, of course, use decorations and mementoes from high school as the centerpieces. Go around the table and ask each guest to share their fondest memory of high school. Take photos of the mother/daughter pairs for take-home treasures to remember this special time.

Oh The Places You'll Go ◎ Your grad will likely receive at least one copy of this Dr. Seuss classic, *Oh, the Places You'll Go!*, so throw a party in true Dr. Seuss style. Use the book as the basis for your invitation. "Oh The Places You'll Go with (your grad's name)." Make an easel sign with a caricature of your grad that says "Congratulations (Grad's name)! Tonight is your night. You're off to great places, so get ready—you're about to take flight!" Guests can leave special messages for the grad. Make a welcome sign with the words "Oh The Places You'll Go, (your grad's name)." In the background have a directional sign showing all the places your grad has been or wants to go. Decorate with balloons in the colors on the book's cover and serve anything green (in the tradition of green eggs) in full Seuss tradition.

It's A Jungle Out There ◎ Host a jungle-themed party for your graduates taking that big step into the "real world." Create centerpieces around the house with stuffed jungle animals. Serve fruity drinks in coconut shells, and carve out pineapples to serve other jungle treats. If you have trees in your yard, tie ropes to strong branches so your graduate guest can swing like Tarzan, or George of the Jungle. Play jungle-themed music, like "The Lion Sleeps Tonight," or "The Banana Boat Song." Host limbo contests and serve tropical punches and loads of animal crackers.

Graduation Gifts

The Big Time ◎ Kindergarten, pre-school, elementary, and middle-school graduations have grown in popularity, as these are big steps for children. Each year of school is a special accomplishment, so give your child something big to celebrate the transition, like a big kids' back-pack, or a big kids' outfit. Plan a day of big kids' fun to celebrate the occasion, but be a kid again, and join in the fun with homemade cup-cakes, and ice cream floats.

Watch Out! ◎ It's graduation time, and for your college graduate's one moment in time, give him or her a watch, or new clock, engraved with the words, "It's time to be out on your own, but please find time call us back home!" You can also give a watch with a note that says, "Let this gift remind you to 'watch out' for our daughter (son, grand-son, etc)!"

Ticket To Ride ◎ Give your graduate a ticket to ride—home, that is! Create a ticket that includes the numbers of airlines that fly between your cities, and include a note that says, "This ticket is good for one ticket to ride . . . back home!"

"Plane" Fun ◎ Your grad worked hard, so give him or her a gift of pure fun. Consider giving a gift card or check to be used toward some "plane" fun. Since graduates are well known for gallivanting from col-lege to college to see friends, or venturing to exotic places or beaches during spring break, the gift of travel to be applied to plane fare, or travel of some kind, will be totally memorable, and put to good use. Find a toy plane, and attach your gift to it for a high-flying delivery.

The T-shirt Quilt ◎ When my friend's son went to college, she got his permission to give away a selection of his prized T-shirts from high school as they cleaned out his room. From rock concerts to sporting events, he had saved well over a hundred shirts, which represented meaningful moments in his life, from soccer teams to camps he at-tended. He never in a million years thought she had something up her sleeve as he parted with these prized tees. As she bagged them up and carted them off, he pleaded to keep just a few more, but she didn't give in. When he came home from college for the holidays, she presented him with the best gift he had ever received. His mom had taken all the T-shirts, cut off the images, and sewn them into a soft, comfortable quilt. He took his prized quilt back to college and was the talk of the dorm. In the event you don't want to make a quilt, a pillow or smaller throw is still a memorable way to preserve those tees.

Spring Break © If everyone is giving the graduate serious gifts, and you want to stand out, fill a toy beach bucket with an assortment of gifts ranging from a colorful beach towel with her name monogrammed on it, to a gift card, or certificate to a video store or fast food restaurant. Add a favorite CD, mp3 player, or whatever is the latest greatest gadget, and fill that bucket with fun and games.

Outstanding In His Field © Tell the graduate he is outstanding in his field, and prepare for him an SOS survival kit for college. This will include everything from quarters for the laundry, an umbrella, flashlight, tool kit for his car, a box of BAND-AIDs, coupons for local pizza delivery, and anything else you can think of that will help him in an emergency situation.

The Gift Of The Butterfly © A college senior named Lindsay Roberts shared a wonderful idea that has meant so much to her over the years. She wrote, "For a few major accomplishments my mom has given me butterfly necklaces. To her the butterfly symbolizes evolving and she gives them to me during transition points in my life. She gave me a gold one for kindergarten graduation, a pearl one for high-school graduation, and a designer one for my twenty-first birthday. Because of this, butterflies have become very inspiring to me."

Job Seeking? © Make a job search kit for a college student or new graduate. Include a notebook or journal for keeping track of activity, a business card holder, and a copy of the book by the leading job fair expert Tory Johnson (that I had the pleasure of co-authoring) called *Women For Hire: The Ultimate Guide to Getting a Job*. For an extra special addition, put all of it in a stylish tote bag or briefcase.

Money Tree © All graduates appreciate money and there are clever and creative ways to give them what they will appreciate most. Buy a photo tree, and transform it with money by inserting the money into the places that a photograph would normally go. Or, if you can't find a money tree, purchase a small bonsai tree, and fan-fold the money, and then pinch it in the middle, and wrap a pipe-cleaner or wire twist around the center of the bill. It will open up like a butterfly—then attach it to the bonsai tree for a fabulous display of green.

Bound Bills © I'll never forget the time our cousin Arlene Hoffman in Houston gave our son a bound stack of clean, new dollar bills. There are many banks across the country that offer pages, or bound packages, so find a source in your area that does this service, and package the bills like a notebook, or pad of paper.

To The Smell Of Success © Find out if your graduate appreciates scented fragrances and, if so, build a themed gift around the idea, "To the sweet smell of your success!" It's easy to do a little research and find out his or her favorite fragrances, brands, hair and beauty products, and more. Anything that smells good is game for your gift. Include a travel or makeup bag for a girl, or a dopp kit for a boy, and even consider monogramming it with his or her name or initials.

A Word From The Wise © Perhaps you know someone famous, or have connections, and can arrange for a call from them to your graduate with a word from the wise. When our son Justin was graduating from college, I was working on an event that had a very famous lawyer in attendance. Since Justin was headed to law school, I asked this gentleman if he would mind talking for a few moments to Justin about becoming a lawyer. He wholeheartedly agreed, and was incredible. When I called Justin and said Johnnie Cochran would like to say hello, at first he didn't believe me. When Justin realized it was really Johnnie Cochran, he just about fainted. It was such a kind deed, and Justin will remember that call forever.

The Graduate's Alphabet © Graduates will appreciate an electronic dictionary, or conversion dictionary in two languages, for a second language course he or she will be taking in college. It's a high-tech toy and a great gift that will be put to good use. To make it especially memorable, include the graduate's alphabet:

A is for Attitude. Have a great one.
B is for Bravo. You really rate one!
C is for Call me—I'll always be there.

D is for Devoted—just know that I care.
E is for Excellent—that's what you are.
F is for Family and Friends—they think you're a star.
G is for Graduation—a look at your past.
H is for Home—please get back here fast.
I is for Intelligent—use that great mind.
J is for Just always be kind.
K is for be Kind every day.
L is for Learn—your grades will pave the way.
M is for Moving—it sure is a trip.
N is for your New surroundings—we hope you will flip.
O is for Outstanding—yes, that's you!
P is for Persistence—in all that you do.
Q is for Quality friends and family who care.
R is for Remember the times that we shared.
S is for Special down to your core,
T is for Terrific times that are in store.
U is for Unforgettable times to treasure.
V is for Victories—too many to measure.
W is for Wonderful—we know you will be.
X is for X-ray every opportunity.
Y is for You make sure to phone.
Z is for Zoom—come quickly back home.

Graduate Thank You's

If you're a graduate, then you'll be writing many thank-you notes to say "thank you for the gifts," and more. Refer to the "U" that is filled with unforgettable words and phrases to express your appreciation. Here's a memorable thank you we received:

Dear Spizman Family,

I just wanted to thank you for the graduation wishes and gift. I will be sure to put the money to good use. Your generosity, like always, is extremely appreciated. It's hard to believe that four years is over since it seems like, only yesterday, I was filling out applications, and visiting various campuses. I am excited about the opportunity to work in a field that I love and will be finally able to begin my career in the movie business. I look forward to maintaining and strengthening our relationship in the future, no matter where I am. Thank you for everything, from your advice, to your help, and extended kindness, I am lucky to know people like you.

Sincerely, Josh Weinstock

Go confidently in the directions of your dreams.

Live the life you've imagined.

—Henry David Thoreau

H

is for Home Sweet Home
and Hostess Gifts

Your home is your palace, your abode, and should be and can be a place where you can create memories, and a special place to escape to. Whenever a home is especially memorable, it is usually because it reflects the person who lives there. Their taste, passion, things they collect, favorite colors, and personality shine through, and provide a lasting impression.

This chapter focuses on everything from announcing your change of address to moving to a new house. You'll also find some creative ways to thank someone for having you to dinner, or entertaining you as a weekend guest. Since no one wants more dust catchers, a thoughtful gift is one they'll put to use and really enjoy. Whatever you choose, be sure to let them know how appreciated they are with a gesture that reflects your good taste as well.

The following ideas are yours for the choosing. Your home sweet home can be memorable and, with a little help from the professionals, you, too, can make a statement that lasts a lifetime.

Moving Announcements

We've moved to somewhere new,
But hope to stay in touch with you!

Here's how to reach us—be sure to know,
We hope you'll come by and soon say hello.

Moving To A New Home

A Memorable Moving Day ⓒ Moving day can move anyone to tears. Not only can it be stressful, but it's tiring as well. Close family members and friends would most likely appreciate a hand, so ease the chaos with a moving-day basket. Fill it with moving supplies, and necessities like snacks, cleaning powders, a few rolls of toilet paper, bottled water, and provide a few extra hands to help unpack.

Hotel Spizman ⓒ If you want to provide a memorable stay at your home, here's how! Whenever we have a guest stay at our house, we think of ourselves as a temporary hotel. On a tray in the bathroom we put little bottles of shampoo, lotion, and a shower cap, as well as a welcome basket filled with bottled water, midnight snacks, and a few magazines that match our guest's interests. I also place a photograph on their nightstand of special times shared with them, and provide a choice of pillows—feather, or foam in case of allergies. We roll out the welcome mat to insure our guest's comfort.

A Gesture That Moved Me ⓒ Richard, a gentleman who recently moved, commented, "People say that moving is traumatic, and I can agree with this assessment. I had recently been diagnosed with a serious illness and was unable to handle the stress of moving." Enter Evelyn. "What made her efforts so memorable was that Evelyn assisted me with loads of calls and contacts to help me line up every detail with my move. So often people give gifts, but she gave the gift of her time, which mattered most. She lined up the moving truck, helped everything get boxed and made me a list of every contact I would need during my move."

A Housewarming ⓒ On the day a fellow co-worker moved in to their new house, one group of teachers sent a basket with breakfast, muffins, lunch, a bouquet of flowers, and a bottle of wine. It was such a lovely gesture, and each teacher sent something in the basket that contributed to the housewarming.

Pantry Party © Instead of a traditional housewarming party where guests often bring bottles of wine, or houseplants, throw your new neighbor a pantry party so they get what they really need. From dish soap to plastic wrap, from chocolate chips to baking soda, ask guests to bring along a pantry essential. Not only will it be fun to celebrate the new digs, but also fun to see what items people consider essential stock.

You Go "Grill" © A recent caller on my *Giftionary* radio show on Star 94 in Atlanta said she wanted to give her mother a grill for her new home. She inquired how to make it more memorable, and that was easy. I said to attach a card to the grill that says, "You go grill!" I also advised she should add a thank-you-style grocery list of all the things she was thankful for that her mother has done for her. Thank her for the endless hugs, hundreds of hamburgers, tons of peanut butter, truckloads of love, etc.

Memorable Homes

Hall Of Fame © Our friend Lynne transformed a hall by creating a wall of family fame in her house. What made it so special was that she thoughtfully selected a photograph of each family member from many generations back. She made sure she also wrote on the back of each framed photograph something special about the family member. Take Lynne's advice, and be sure to list the names and something about each person—be it their birth date, or how they are related—to provide a keepsake to treasure forever.

Suits You To A Tea © Everyone loves my friend Patty's teacup and saucer collection, which is beautifully displayed in an antique china cabinet. Each teacup has sentimental value, since she was given many of the cups from family members. Knowing how much she adores her collection, searching for special ones became a meaningful treasure hunt when searching for a gift for Patty. In fact, my most memorable gift to her was a teacup that I found while antiquing, and it had on it one word written in gold script. The word was, *Friend*. It had Patty's name all over it.

A Taste Of Home ⓒ Homesick friend, or relative far away? Send something unique from home. A friend from New England moved to Texas where the leaves do not change. Her mother sent her a box of colored leaves as a surprise treat. A native Texan now in Georgia gets real Tex-Mex tamales and corn tortillas from his home, and one aunt sends her niece real Eastern Carolina barbeque-on-ice every fall. Whether it's key limes and citrus from Florida, Chicago pizza, or sand and shells from a California beach, the distance gap closes with a hometown treat.

A Silver Spoon Surprise ⓒ Margaret Lawson preserved her three generations of baby spoons in a meaningful way—in a beautiful wooden spoon rack that she displays in her powder room. The wall shelf holds all three generations of spoons, including her father's silver spoon from 1934. Each spoon has little dents, because they were actually used to eat porridge and cereal. The spoons continue to be a conversation piece for everyone who visits her powder room, an unlikely place to store such a lovely surprise.

Garage Galore ⓒ Joan Weiss has a garage like no other on earth. Not only did she air-condition and heat it, but she also had the garage painted a bright color and puts indoor-and-outdoor carpet on the floor when she entertains. Her grandchildren enjoy it year-round when it's raining, since they roller-skate in it when the weather is bad. She also hangs artwork in the garage to give it a special flair. Talk about making use of every space creatively!

To A Tee ⓒ My friend Ava gave her husband Bob a memorable gift on his fiftieth birthday: she surprised him with a putting green in the backyard that has five holes, one for each decade of his life. She hired a company to do this, and the entire green was maintenance-free due to the materials used. She told him he was a hole-in-one husband, and it's still one of his favorite gifts of all time.

Fit To Be Framed ⓒ A frame provides instant opportunities for making memories. I've framed everything from my toy puppets from childhood and my first baby dress, to my grandmother's beaded purse. It's a wonderful way to preserve something special and allows you to live creatively with meaningful items while adding a decorative statement.

Hostess Gifts

All In One Gift © One of my close friends, who has us to dinner often, always says, "never to bring a thing," but I never listen. In fact, I usually figure out something she flips over and we both have a good laugh. Last weekend was one of those occasions, and since it was her birthday, it was easy to surprise her with a birthday cake. To top it off, though, I brought a silver cake server to serve it, and a cake plate that matched her china. I also threw in the happy birthday plates, so the gift came totally equipped.

Five Fabulous Things . . . You Can't Live Without © This is as much fun to give a hostess entertaining you as it is to buy: Think of five of your favorite things, the most fabulous things you love, enjoy, and just couldn't live without. For one person, that's a certain magazine, and for another, it's a gadget. It can be anything you just adore. Fill a box, or basket, or bag with these items, and a note that says, "Here are six fabulous things I can't live without. You already know you're the first!"

Noticeable Napkins © Napkins might sound common, but all you need to do to make them memorable is paint them with fabric paints, and in a pretty script write different sayings, or the family, or individual's name, or initials.

Follow Me © We all try to be neighborly, but sometimes more is called for. If a neighbor has an emergency, death, or illness in the family, and has to be away, make their return as easy as possible. Mow the lawn, water the flowers, gather the mail and papers, and then, when they return, have a red ribbon tied to the front door, with a note saying, "Follow me." The ribbon will lead to your house, where you'll have dinner waiting along with disposable containers, so they can take it home. Keep it simple, be sympathetic, but not intrusive, and they'll thank you for your consideration.

Getting To Know You © When a new neighbor moves in, everybody brings cookies and a smile. But a really thoughtful neighbor can show up with a list of handymen, phone numbers for the schools, police, churches, synagogues, locations of grocery stores and gas stations, directions to the mall and the post office, and recommendations of doctors and dentists. Along with your list, offer a guided tour of the city at their convenience, showing them the athletic arenas, where the little league plays, how to get downtown, how to get to public transportation, where the best shopping is, how to get to museums, the zoo, farmers' market, and anything else they care to know about. You can also surprise them with a personalized or pretty doormat. Attach a card that reads, "We just wanted to roll out the welcome mat!"

Spreading Good Cheer ◎ Tory Johnson suggested giving this hostess gift during the holiday season. "Pick up individual vintage jam spreaders from a flea market (they're often available at a bargain, as singles without a set), or purchase new ones at any specialty store. Use a ribbon to attach the spreader to a jar of your favorite gourmet jam or chocolate sauce. Attach a note saying, "Spread good cheer in the New Year."

A Handful of Thanks ◎ A memorable way to give a gift, when staying at someone's house, is to leave it on the dresser, or nightstand. If you fear they'll see it before you go, place it in the closet, and leave behind a treasure-hunt clue where to find it. Discovering your gift after you've left will be a wonderful surprise. If you want to really be creative, you can bring monogrammed hand towels, and leave them on the counter with a note of thanks that says, *I've got to hand it to you, you're the best hostess on earth!*

Next Morning Gift ◎ If you attend a dinner party, here's a creative idea: bring a gift that will be enjoyed the morning after. Fill a basket with breakfast goodies, including bagels, jams, pastries and muffins. Add a note that says, *Thanks for good food, friends, and laughter. Enjoy this basket the morning after!*

Pet Gifts ◎ Pets are valued family members. If your hostess has a pet, focus your gift on their four-legged friend. From dog or cat treats, to creative food bowls, and toys, this is a thoughtful way to say "thank you," or express your appreciation. You could also take your own snapshots of their pet and surprise them with copies in your thank-you note. It's definitely a way to make a memorable statement.

I

is for Inviting Invitations

An invitation is the first impression you make when inviting guests to a party or special event. From that first moment when opening the envelope, to RSVPing that they will be delighted to attend, an invitation is the first of many memories that you can make for a special event or party. The goal in creating a memorable invitation is to begin your mission at your guest's first glance.

Celebrated invitation artist and designer Gwen Ware, owner of The Electronic Pencil, custom-designs unusually creative, keepsake-quality invitations that are individually handcrafted. Gwen feels that to be memorable, an invitation must stand out from all the other mail and say "Look at me, FIRST!" and that the look and feel of a memorable invitation instantly differentiates it from your everyday mail, or even other invitations. To Gwen, invitations are an art form. Having created invitations for many celebrities and well-known companies, Gwen's invitations scream *special,* and she shared some of her creative ideas.

VIP Invitation Tips

• When composing the invitation's text, choose clever words that capture the imagination.

• Select a descriptive graphic from your invitation's design and print it on the mailing envelope. This elevates the importance of the envelope from just part of the invitation's delivery system to an important component of the invitation's design. It also gives the guest a foretaste of the invitation inside.

- Don't create an irritating cleanup problem for yourself, your guests, or the post office by placing confetti or glitter inside the envelopes.

- To create a "pulled together" look, use the same font that you used on the invitation to print guest names and addresses on the mailing envelopes.

- When you want an invitation to stand out and be noticed, choose envelopes whose color, size, or shape are unique.

- When addressing envelopes, print guest names and addresses in very large letters by setting the font size to eighteen or higher. Guests love seeing their names and addresses prominently featured on envelopes; it makes them feel special.

- Search for a postage stamp that reflects your theme or whose colors complement the invitation. Trim the serrated edges for a detail that's over the top, or check to see if you can order trimmed stamps from your post office.

- If you decide to make your envelopes, never use too much glue. Leave a small opening without glue at the start of the flap so that it's easy to slip a finger in the corner and open it up. Try opening the envelope after sealing it to make sure it opens easily. Or, check out Velcro resealing dots that are adhesive and allow you to open and close the invitation without ripping the envelope.

- Always arrange to have invitations hand cancelled to avoid having the post office's machinery print black tracking marks on the envelopes. It is courteous to telephone the manager of the local post office in advance and arrange a time and day to have the invitations hand cancelled.

All of these little details truly matter. Really creative and memorable invitations have a unique personality and an element of surprise. The theme, papers, colors, textures, types of ink, graphics, words, and presentation combine to make a statement. One of Gwen's exceptionally creative invitations was designed for a surprise birthday party that a Florida socialite planned for her husband. Since the party's décor and food were to be Oriental in style, Gwen created a colorful miniature Oriental kite, printed on Japanese Unryu paper, and mounted on wooden sticks, as the birthday invitation. The invitation to attend the party was printed on the kite's tail. Best of all, if the kite was bowed, it would fly! The invitation's copy read:

Honored Friend
We humbly invite you
To attend a
Far-Out
Far-East
Surprise Party!

More Tips From Gwen For Making Plain Invitations Memorable ©

- Consider the guest of honor's personality and interests, and choose one concept or theme you want your invitation to communicate. For ideas, check out the person's clothing style, hobbies, passions, favorite sayings, mannerisms, or favorite colors, and have the invitation reflect their personality.

- Don't be afraid to create invitations using textured papers. Textures add pizzazz to invitations. You can create wonderful textured invitations by printing the invitation's text on translucent vellum paper and placing it on top of the textured paper. Consider using raffia, ribbon, cord, colorful twist-ties or novel paper clips to bind the two sheets together.

- Transform an ordinary invitation with a gold or silver magic marker by running the tip of the marker along the edge of the invitation. Don't worry about it being straight since it will look handcrafted. Just like the pros!

- When creating cards from artist's watercolor paper, think how you'll show off those beautiful, uneven edges in the invitation's design; deckled edges add interest.

- Experiment with origami—it's the key to unusual and exciting invitations. You'll be surprised how many options you have with invitations and ways to fold paper.

- Use a variety of objects and materials to decorate the invitation. Use found objects, from buttons, to odds and ends, to stamp shapes. Explore different everyday objects to glue inside.

- Have fun exploring and experimenting with paper of all types, including office paper, butcher's paper, gift wrap, parchment, paper towels, and cardboard. Fold it, sew it with a zigzag stitch, splatter-paint it, tie-dye it, batik, crimp, rip it, dip it, and snip it into unusual shapes.

- Don't stop there . . . from fabric, to cereal boxes, toys, gift boxes, and more, you have endless choices for creative invitations. Just go shopping at a close-out store, or toy, or dime store. You'll be surprised at all your inviting options.

- Create beautiful cards by tearing them from paper by hand, rather than creating an artificially straight edge using scissors or a paper cutter.

And don't forget: When throwing a surprise party for any age, be sure to go to the trouble to create a fake invitation under false pretense so that your guest of honor will be totally shocked when he or she arrives and finds the party is really for him or her.

First Impressions Count

An Address Addition © The first thing your guests will see is their addressed invitation upon delivery. To make a memorable impression, one of my favorite ideas is to write something special about the individuals under their name. Instead of just writing "Mr. and Mrs. Jack Freedman" and then the address, I add a special compliment or detail about them such as "World's Greatest Grandparents." The invitation puts a smile right on their face even before they open up the invitation and find out more.

And The Envelope Please ◎ To create some mailbox drama, add a detail, icon, sticker, or something special on the envelope. Vary the shape of your envelope, use a color scheme that's eye-catching, and consider how to grab the attention of your recipient, and the mailman, too!

Hand-Canceled Stamps ◎ If you've ever seen a beautiful invitation printed in stunning calligraphy, and then unsightly black track marks running across the front of the envelope, that means the envelope ran through a machine to cancel the stamp. To avoid these unwelcome marks on your invitation, visit your local post office, and ask for permission to hand cancel your stamps. This takes extra time, but is well worth it, and most post offices offer this option. The hand-canceler is a little gadget that puts a neat cancel right over the stamp and doesn't interfere with the rest of the envelope.

An RSVP To Remember ◎ One of my favorite ideas for a memorable RSVP is to list on your invitation your telephone number, but make it a second, or separate, line. Record a fabulous message that reflects the theme of the party. Get super-creative and play a song that fits the party theme, and include a poem like:

Thank you for your RSVP,
At a fabulous party you soon will be.
Leave your name and a yes or no,
And the number of people who will show.

Creative Invitations

What's in a name? ◎ Everything, if you spend a few minutes getting creative. Here are some inventive ways to incorporate the guest of honor's name in your invitation. Build the theme around his or her John Hancock for a personal touch. Here's how:

Always In Love With Amy (Abby, Ali, Annie)
For Our Jack-Of-All-Trades
You're Just-in Time! Justin's party is right around the corner!
Less is More! Find out how "much" more at his 55th birthday party!

I Love Lucy, Lori, Lara, Lois, Linda . . . etc.
She's Marla–vous! Come help us celebrate her big day!
Jules Of The Night
Alyson Wonderland
By golly—Molly is Seven!
It's Even-Steven—He's 44!
Our Lisa will be all smiles!
I D'Claire—Look who is aging!
Can you Beli–eva Eva's Turning 50?
Calling All of Anne's Fans!
Everyone Loves Raymond (Ray, Ralph)

Some Birthday Invitations ©

1st Birthday

We're having a party and tons of fun,
Because _____ is turning one!

(Western Party)
Ride 'em cowboy to my party,
From _____ To _____, you'll chow down hearty.
I'm rounding up my friends for some birthday fun,
At my corral 'cause I'm turning ONE!
Bring your mom and bring your dad,
For the best ole time you've ever had.
Happy Trails! Dress:Western

2nd Birthday

Everyone is welcome, it will be a zoo,
Calling all party animals—_____ is turning two!

Baah Baah, Oink, Meow and Moo,
_____ is turning two!

We're having a party and we're inviting guess who?
Come for ice cream and cake because _____ is turning two!

(Ballerina Party)
We're "tutu" excited.
_____ is turning two!

3rd Birthday

I'm having a party and turning three,
Hope you'll come and party with me.

Wear your very best and prettiest pearls,
We're having a party just for girls.
Please dress like Mommy and don't be late,
We'll see you on _____—let's make it a date!

4th Birthday

(Tea Party)
Come for cake and a little tea,
Because _____ is turning three.

(Pirate Party)
Ahoy there mates—a party is in store,
Because _____ is turning four.

(Trucks)
Truckloads of fun, cake, and prizes galore,
Steer your way to _____'s party and help him "turn" four.

(Magic Party)
Magic, prizes, much, much more!
_____ is turning four.

5th Birthday

(Swimming Party)
You'll swim, play games, eat cake, and jive,
Splish, splash, _____ is turning five.

It's A Pirate Party!
Skull-bones, skeletons, man alive,
Call out the Pirates . . . because _____ is five.
A treasure hunt and treats galore,
Come help _____ say good-bye to four!

6th Birthday

Mountains of food, oceans of fun,
It's _____'s sixth birthday, and we guarantee fun!

Say CHEESE! (Pizza, that is!)
And Join _____
For A Birthday Pizza Party.

(Dancing Party)
_____ *is doing leaps and twirls,*
It's her 6th birthday, and we're inviting all girls!

7th Birthday
Seven is a lucky number,
and _____ *will feel lucky, too,*
If you attend his seventh birthday,
since he's lucky to know you!

(High Tea)
Put on your finest hat and set of pearls,
We're having a tea party just for girls.

8th Birthday
We hope you'll join us and celebrate,
Since _____ *is officially turning eight.*

Slide into home and have some cake,
Your pal _____ *is aiming at eight.*

Tween Parties (Ages 9–12) ©

9th Birthday
We really think it'd be so fine,
If you'd join _____ *skating (rock climbing, etc.) since she (he) is*
   turning nine.

10th Birthday
(Party at a Beauty or Nail Salon)
It's a Glamour Girl Party and we're calling all cuties,
Please join _____ *for a day of beauty!*

(Sports Party)
It's a grand slam party, come dressed to play ball,
_____ *is turning ten, and that's the referee's call!*

(Pottery Party, Art Party)
We hope you're feeling a little arty,
Since it's _____ *'s birthday and we're throwing a party.*

11th to 12th Birthday

It's A No-Slumber Party!
You are officially invited to not slumber!
But if you prefer to sleep, only sweet dreams are allowed!
Fun around the clock with _____'s entire crowd.

(Pinball Wizard)
It's a video-game party, come try your hand,
_____ is turning _____, and the party will be grand.

Teenage Parties ©

Beach Bash. Send an invitation written with a permanent marker on a plastic beach ball that is not inflated. Include the instruction to inflate this invitation to read.

Sweet Sixteen—License To Party. Send out a license to party with your birthday honoree. Pattern it after a driver's license, and fill in all the details to fit. Fill in each guest's name on the license with the time, date, and location of the party.

We Reserved a Spot Just For You! From polka-dotted shoes, to handbags, the spotted theme is a fun invitation to search for, or create for, a teenage girl. Polka dots are always in style, so they'll be easy to add, or find, to get your point across.

Adult Parties ©

Bowl Him Over! Here's a poem perfect for a bowling birthday bash:
Let's bowl _____ over,
And give him a surprise,
His birthday's rolling closer
And he's striking 35!
Spare us, please come
Help ease his aging pain.
Wish him years of happiness
As he's headed down the lane!

"On Broadway" Party. Theater. Reviews. Create a playbill invitation that has all the information centered around your favorite play. For example, "Mamma Mia—Phyllis is turning 75!" Whatever the theme of your show is, create the invitation, and serve food to match. Name each course based on the acts, and play the sound-track to set the mood.

Here's The Deal. And it's for Gamblers Only. Include a deck of cards, or mount the invite onto a playing card with a brad that attaches it. Invite guests to try their hand at partying!

50's Finest. This one's easy to pull off when you send an invitation that is actually a list of the top forty songs that played in the fifties. Do a little research, and throw a sock-hop, complete with hamburgers, milk shakes, and a jukebox or DJ. Or, find a photo strip, he or she did as a teenager, like the ones from the minute-made, old-fashioned, black-and-white photo booths, and incorporate that into the invitation.

Lorie turning Fifty? IM-PASTA-BLE! Send out an Italian-themed dinner party invitation and use this phrase on the invitation.

Forever Young! That's what this invitation will say as you list all the latest skin-care remedies, and include a few samples from your local department store to set the stage for a wrinkle-free party.

S. S. Spizman. The S. S. Spizman is ready to sail, so create an invite around this nautical theme. Toy ships filled with munchies, casual dress, and sailor hats, sunglasses, and sunscreen make this a perfect party.

We'll Party To A Tee. Send out this message with all the details about the party printed on a T-shirt. Guests will be so surprised when their invite comes printed on the T-shirt.

Surprise Fiftieth Party
Shhh . . . don't tell _____,
Her party is a surprise.
Bring a roast or bring a toast
And leave home all the guys!

Luau
It's a Hawaiian Five–oh! Party.

Baseball theme
_____ is at bat,
And it's the top of his 5th decade!

Horse-racing Theme

_____ *is out in front fifty lengths!*

Golf

Come watch _____
as he begins his senior tour!

A Party To Remember. When my beloved grandmother Pauline turned eighty-six, it was the same month our daughter, Ali, turned one. So, we had their birthday parties together. It was such a meaningful event, and the invitation read:

We're having a birthday—it'll be quite a mix,
Because Ali's turning one and Grandma Pauline eighty-six.
So join us for cake and come for the fun,
Celebrate Grandma's big birthday and Ali's little one.

Have A Pet Party. Have a pet birthday party. Invite all of your friends and their dogs, too. Center everything around a dog theme—dog-bone-shaped cake for the people, and doggie ice cream bowls topped with dog bones for the canine cavorters. Create games for the dogs and their owners to do together and give dog-themed treat bags with fun items for the furry friends. Take loads of photographs, and give them to your friends all year long for special occasions.

Anniversary Invitations

Anniversary Parties ©

We won't be serving oysters Rockefeller,
But we promise the company will be stellar.
We're having a cookout and hope you can come,
To witness twenty-five years of marital fun.

Marriage Certificate. Photocopy their marriage certificate, and superimpose the invitation right on the information. Then duplicate it for a fun invite and help the happy couple re-create their special day.

Invitations For Other Events

Halloween ©

It's a Baby Boo–mers Ball!

Christmas ©

Jingle Bells, Jingle Bells,
Jingle all the way,
We're having a holiday party
And hope you'll come and stay!

Chanukah ©

(Illustrate a spinning dreidel)
We're spinning out of control!
Join us for a Chanukah party!
The fun begins here.

Engagement ©

_____ *is feeling really sweet,*
Because she knocked _____ *off his feet.*
We hope you'll join us to wish them well
They're getting hitched and we think that's swell!

Couples Wedding Shower ©

Linens to houseware items,
Big and small,
_____ *and* _____
Need it all!

Baby Showers ©

Boy or girl?
Pink or blue
If we only knew!
We're having a shower
And inviting you!

Couples Baby Shower ◎

First they found each other,
Then came marriage.
And soon they'll be pushing,
A baby carriage!

Generic Baby Theme ◎

From booties to bibs,
Blankets, clothing, and more,
Let's shower _____
With presents galore.

Moving Announcements

We've Moved ◎

(cow themes)
We're Mooooo-ving!
Setting up a new pasture at _____.
Hope you'll visit us soon or we'll have a cow!

We've Had A Moving Experience!
Our new address is

_____.

Out Of The Box Announcement ◎ Print your invitation on corrogated cardboard for a fabulous moving announcement that screams moving! Test one piece to make sure it goes through the mail, and then print or write with a permanent black marker your new address. Consider these words:

We've moved!
You'll find us unpacking at

_____..

(state your new address)

Dress—What to Wear—What To Say? ◎

Black Tie, Red Tie, No Tie
Totally Glamorous

Caribbean Casual
Texas Comfortable
No Ties—No Jeans
Fifties Finest—Cocktail Chic
Whatever Makes You Happy
The Scene Is Jeans
Nothing fancy, Nothing too fine—Please just be right on time!
Dress: Surprise us!
Dress: Yes, please! Anything goes!
Anything goes except jeans

Play On Words

As you select a theme for your party or special event, here are some plays on words to help you add a special touch of pizzazz to your party.

Theme: Animals, Jungle Party ©

This is just "fur" you!
You're my "per–fur'd" friend
Have a roaring good time
Have a "bone–afied" Happy Birthday
I can't "bear" to be without you
I'm wild about you
This place is a zoo
I love you "beary" much
Party Animals
I love you and I'm not "lion"
Don't chicken out
Birds of a feather stick together
You make me go ape
Let's monkey around
There's a special spot in my heart
You're my wild thing
There's no "bunny" like you!

Sports ©

It's a kick-off party!
We're kicking off the new year
_____ has scored a touchdown
It's a home-run happening!
_____ is turning fifty and is in the home stretch!
We're having a ball!
Come by for a "short stop" and wish _____ a happy birthday!
It's a chill-out party!
We're in the game
Calling all players
It's a grand slam birthday

The world is so full of a number of things,
I'm sure we should all be as happy as kings.
—Robert Louis Stevenson

J

is for Just Get Well Soon and Notes Of Sorrow

When someone you care about is ill, or recovering from an operation, expressing your concern for his well-being is so meaningful. Whether you send a card, a poem, a gift, or dinner, whatever you do will be greatly appreciated as you offer comfort and concern. When someone is very ill, it's a time when they need privacy, however, I've always learned that you can respect someone's need for space while still expressing your wishes for their recovery. To do so in a meaningful way is key, and there are many ways you can accomplish this.

Discovering what will be memorable and significant takes a little research, but when you find out what will really lift up their spirits, the healing process begins and your ongoing care and concern exceeds any gift you could possibly give. Throughout the years, I've learned that you can never do too much for someone who is going through a difficult time. When acknowledging someone's pain due to the loss of a loved one, just letting them know how much you care is significant enough. You don't have to justify someone's death or offer profound words of wisdom. A caring heart, listening ear, and shoulder to lean on are most meaningful.

The following ideas will help you express your get-well wishes and feelings. To brighten the day of someone who is ill or to touch another's spirit who is grieving is an ongoing gift whose value is priceless.

Get-Well Gifts And Deeds

Dinner To Their Door ◎ Mitzi Kahn of Dallas shared a gift idea she had for a friend who was in the hospital having knee replacement surgery. She decided that instead of just bringing him something that he neither needed, nor would be able to enjoy right after surgery, she'd try something a little different. She and her husband took him a menu from a popular restaurant, and had him circle his food choices for a dinner for he and his wife, to be delivered to his home when he got out of the hospital. They absolutely adored the idea, and were able to enjoy a delicious dinner a week later when he was feeling better and could pay more attention to this thoughtful gesture.

A Garden Of Wishes ◎ Do what one group did for their friend who was bedridden from an operation and dealing with ongoing chemotherapy. Her bedroom overlooked the backyard and this was her pride and joy before she fell ill. The group planted her dwindling garden with beautiful flowers, and came over every other day to maintain it. Just knowing that her beloved garden was being cared for and flourishing was a gift that surrounded her with blooms of love and affection.

Begin A We Love You Fund ◎ If you know a family who is going through a difficult time, due to an illness, and is faced with ongoing major medical expenses, and constant travel, a great idea is to collect greeting cards and donations and create a *We Love You* Fund. Enlist as many friends, acquaintances, business associates, and hometown heroes as you can to send a card filled with get-well wishes and a designated check amount, and send it with love from the group. Wrap it up in a colorful box, and include a letter on top of the box that states they can only accept it with one condition—no thank-you notes allowed! Include one card with your address and a stamp, and tell them to write you back and let you know how things are going, and you will photocopy the message, and distribute it to everyone in the group. This thoughtful gift and wishes from the entire city will be a gift they'll deeply appreciate.

It's In The Cards ◎ Buy a slew of cards and send one every other day. This is one of the most memorable things you can do. The secret to making it really memorable, however, is to give your cards a clever theme. It might be news of the day, or something fun and positive about friends of yours that has happened. Or, a quote for the day that's inspiring and meaningful. Or, do what Betty Storne did for a friend she had heard was ill. She told her she was sending a get well card every month until she actually got well! A year's worth of cards later, her friend's health had greatly improved and, to this day, she continues to remind Bettye how much her monthly get well greeting cards meant.

Etched In Time ◎ When our dear friend Larry's mother became very ill, we created a gift that we hoped would have lasting meaning. His mother, Hannah, didn't want any gifts or flowers, so we really had to be creative. Since one thing Hannah valued most was a love of words, we thought perhaps that would be the right gift. Hannah prided herself on writing poetry, and not an occasion went by without her putting pen to paper. A fan of her poems throughout the years, we had saved quite a few. One in particular stood out—she had written it on the occasion of her ninetieth birthday, and it seemed to be good advice to return to Hannah during her final days. We took the poem to an engraving shop to have her words etched for all time and mounted on a lovely plaque. Hannah thanked us repeatedly for this gift, even when she was too weak to talk, to express how it really touched her heart. Hannah passed away weeks later. She was a special women who will be greatly missed. She gave me permission to share her poem, and it reads as follows:

> As I approached my 90th year
> I sat, contemplated and feared
> That perhaps I should try to run
> Because the best is <u>not</u> yet to come.
> On second thought I think I should stay
> To meet "head on" another day,
> A day of good things, good people and such
> Of all of that I can't have too much.
> —Hannah Brown, 1910–2003

TV Lovers ☺ Is someone you know recuperating from a recent illness and stuck at home? Create a to-do bag and fill it with ways she can pass the time. Purchase a TV Guide, and highlight all of your favorite hot shows, and air-times. Add a few best-selling books on tape, and how about a video of a week's worth of your favorite talk show!

A Little R&R ☺ When a friend of Joan Weiss's in Memphis was not feeling up to par, Joan invited her over and made sure they had a few hours to spend together. Instead of going shopping, or killing time, Joan planned a really kind deed. She hired a massage therapist to be at her house waiting for her friend. When she arrived, Joan surprised her friend with this luxurious pampering, and her friend was so appreciative of this magnanimous gesture.

Get-Well Words ☺ Write a poem from the depths of your heart to wish someone well. Here's an example of a poem that one woman wrote when a family member's mother was ill.

> *We're sending you our deepest thoughts*
> *To brighten up your day.*
> *And let you know how much you're missed*
> *And loved in every way.*
> *We're sending you our heartfelt thoughts*
> *Hoping you'll get well with time.*
> *And packing hugs and kisses, too,*
> *Inside this little rhyme.*

A Get-Well Thank You ☺ When a friend was recovering from an illness, her husband wrote us a poem that was so touching, it was meant to be shared:

> *You who ran to help us,*
> *To you a debt is owed;*
> *And needy as we were my friends,*
> *You lightened our heavy load.*
> *While through your deeds of loving kindness*
> *Love's lessons we have learned;*
> *Your deeds will always be treasured*
> *Our grateful hearts are what you've earned.*

Sorrow

Words Of Love © Whenever someone loses a loved one, and the person is close to the family, we immediately write a letter of condolence. If it's a close friend or family member, we deliver it personally. What I have learned over time is that when you first hear of someone's passing, it means so much if you immediately respond before the masses of condolence cards pour in. If your children also knew the person or family, it is very special to have them draw a picture, or send a card as well. Since our children were little, we encouraged them to put their feelings into words, and to this day they are comfortable expressing their feelings to family and friends in a meaningful way.

Plant A Tree © Plant a tree and plant a thoughtful gesture. While it might seem like a common thing to do, when I've had a tree planted in a forest in their loved one's name, those grieving often said this small act had a big impact. From planting trees in a forest in a faraway country, like Israel, to a tree at your local church, there are many options available.

The Memory Cake © When you're having a get-together or, especially, a family reunion, do what one family did to pay tribute to those who had passed away and were no longer present. When they celebrated all the birthdays that occurred that year with a giant cake, they also brought out a small cake, with a single candle lit, to commemorate the loved ones that were no longer with them. This meant so much to the family members who had lost loved ones, since the family reunion was a constant reminder of who was missing. This little deed was deeply appreciated, and reminded everyone of the lives of those relatives who had passed away, and the roles they played, and their contributions to the family. When lighting the memory cake, as they called it, they said a beautiful tribute about each person, addressing how they brightened the family with their love, and how much they are missed.

A Funeral To Remember © Deedee Chereton, who recently lost her beloved ninety-four-year-old mother, wanted to make her mom's funeral extra special, and so she printed a memorial booklet that each person received as they arrived at the funeral. It included a poem that her mother, Mrs. Hannah Jacobs, had been given on the occasion of her eighty-fifth birthday. It was a touching tribute to a warm and remarkable woman to celebrate her life.

On Her 85th Birthday . . .
She was the eldest of Gert and Gibby and Buster,
Who gave Sam and Sophie a family of luster.
Blonde curls and blue eyes and a pretty young smile,
A girl of true substance, beyond all denial.

She's a woman of style, plays the ivories by ear,
But above all other things, she holds family most dear;
From Deedee and Sheila, to Roy and the rest—
Her secret to life? It's the oatmeal (we guess).

So we ask you to join in our birthday commotion,
To celebrate joy and boundless devotion.
A love that could reach from Taiwan to Savannah,
Yet could not match the treasure we have in dear Hannah.

A Caretaker's Touching Goodbye © After the death of Deedee Chereton's mother, one letter in particular deeply touched Deedee, and became a treasured gift. Six caretakers shared her mother's shift over the course of many years, and an important part of their job was the extensive documentation in a composition logbook detailing her daily care. When her mother passed away, one of the caretakers came by four days after the funeral, and told Deedee that she never got the chance to say good-bye, and requested if she could write her final farewell letter in the logbook. The letter was so beautiful it was meant to be included in this book, too:

Sunday, July 6th, 2003

Hello Mrs. Jacobs.

I have come to say good-bye and it's not the same. The flowers were beautiful, and they look so refreshed and calm, as if you had something to do with that; but I wasn't able to see those big blue eyes. That's OK though. I want to thank you for being so sweet, nice, and understanding when I was late. For asking about the children and for your wisdom and your compas-

sion towards all of us, because we know you were tired of being turned and everything we did to disturb your peaceful view out of the window.

I remember when I came in you would say, There's Reese, before I would get through the door, and as soon as we were face-to-face you would say, "Hello Darling, how was your bus ride?" I remember the southern lady who knew every birthday, every name and every time it was time to come and go! I learned patience and respect from you. I know it took a lot of patience to deal with the different nurses that came and went and you gave us all respect. I hope I can hang on to all of that as I continue to mature in life. You are missed but will always be remembered.

Deedee made sure everything was just as you would have liked it. The family came together as one and the rabbi said some wonderful things. The girls explained you well. I want to say Bye-Bye sweetheart, have a safe and wonderful journey. Always come through and let us know you're around, and stay that respectful, beautiful and compassionate Southern Belle that I got to know.

I love You. Peace be unto you,
Your friend,
Larysse

> The best way to cheer yourself up
> is to try to cheer somebody else up.
> —Mark Twain

K

is for Kids and
Making Memories

On every occasion or event in a child's life there is a chance to build meaningful memories. Think back to your own childhood. What are some of your favorite memories that come to mind? From holiday memories, to sharing time with friends or family, our lives are a kaleidoscope of memories. When creating memorable moments, it's the little things over the years that will ultimately mean the most. In fact, some memories are so special that they become traditions your children will share with their children. So consider making a commute to school, an outing to the grocery, or just dinner at your favorite restaurant a time to make memories, and enjoy every single second!

What's really special about making memories with kids, is that you also have an opportunity to share important values, and things that you hold close to your heart. You have a way to encourage positive behavior, really get to know your child, and find new ways to connect. From volunteering or doing for others, to simply sharing family time and strengthening bonds, making memories is a way to let a child know that you love them unconditionally with all your heart and soul. Memory-making also reminds children that they are special and appreciated. Let them know they are loved from the sun to the moon and back. This chapter presents some creative ways to accomplish that memory-making goal.

Good-Manners Night ⊚ One family I know has a "good-manners night" once a week. Instead of correcting their young children constantly, which was making dinner unpleasant, they designated one night during the week to practice good table manners. Practice might make perfect, but Good-Manners Night actually made it a lot of fun for everyone involved.

The Grade Fairy ⊚ Nancy Joffre shared a clever idea with me about school. She wrote: "A wise friend once told me that the beginning of each school year, when children are younger, is a great time to try to break old habits and begin new ones. So the night before my daughter started kindergarten, I left a little present and a note from 'The Kindergarten Fairy' by her bed. The note talked about how important it was for kindergarteners to listen, eat their vegetables, go to bed on time, take care of their little sister or brother, etc . . . It introduced the 'Kindergarten Fairy' as someone who would be watching her and was so proud of all she had accomplished, and it also reassured her that kindergarten was sure to be fabulous."

Scribble ⊚ With a black pen, marker, or crayon, quickly scribble a line all over a piece of paper, and then challenge your child to transform it into a drawing. This is a memorable game I loved playing when I was little. By adding eyes, arms, and lots of details I'd turn the scribbles into clowns, monsters—you name it! It is also a great boredom-buster a child can play by herself.

The Thank You Company ⊚ When our daughter Ali was three years old, we appointed her CEO of a pretend family company called The Thank You Company. Ali's job was to acknowledge and "hire" all the nice, caring, kindhearted people we met while doing errands. Not only is this a fun way to teach kindness and good manners, but to top it off, Ali (who is now a teenager) enjoys expressing her gratitude so much, she wrote a book about inventive ways to say "thank you." As the author of *The Thank You Book For Kids: Hundreds of Creative, Cool and Clever Ways to Say Thank You!* she has helped thousands of kids across the country spread their thanks in memorable ways.

The Baby Sitter Bag © Have a separate bag of toys set aside for when the babysitter arrives, and let the kids choose a favorite game, or other items, to be included in the bag. Your children will especially look forward to the babysitter's arrival since they also get to play with her as they enjoy the contents in the bag. It's a great way to structure your child's time, and give everyone an incentive to get along and play constructively.

Dinner Talk © Here's an idea we had that added a memorable twist to our family dinners. We selected a book the entire family enjoyed and, before dinner began, while everyone was just sitting down to the table, we turned off the TV, radio, and any other distractions, and read a few pages out loud to the entire family. Then we enjoyed a group discussion about the content during the meal.

A Family Holiday © Proclaim a special date as your own family holiday; a day of celebration, commemoration, and inspiration. This day could also be a tribute to honor a family member no longer present. Make your family holiday a day of times shared, when you proclaim your love for each other and plan special activities to promote togetherness.

A Party With Heart © Instead of just having a birthday party for your child, plan a party with a meaningful purpose (prior discussion with your child is required). Check with a local children's hospital, homeless shelter, or senior citizens home, and throw a special party for the patients, or residents. This is one of the nicest things your child can do. Invite a small number of kids to help at the party. Make sure every child has a specific job and knows what to do. These jobs range from giving out cupcakes, to leading a sing-a-long, or a talent show put on by the kids.

On The Grow © Lori Simon shared a special idea she had to celebrate her three children. "When my children were little I made up a bulletin board for each of them. Each board, labeled with their name, holds pictures of them at birth, three months, six months, nine months, and then twelve months. It is so amazing to see the changes in that one year! At each of their first birthday parties, I put their board up on an easel and displayed their growth up until that point. So many years later, the boards still hang, and we love to look at them."

Centerpiece Snacks ◎ A fun idea I had, that I always enjoyed doing, was to fill a container with snacks and place it on the kitchen table when our kids had friends over. Our kids helped choose the snacks, and I made sure there was a balance between fruit and other healthy (but kid-approved) treats. This centerpiece of snacks saved the pantry from being raided, and also controlled the junk food consumption. This idea also worked well when a baby-sitter was coming.

The Icing On The Cake ◎ Since our daughter Ali loves to bake, and makes cakes for every occasion and as gifts, I asked my friend Marianne, who is a wonderful baker, if she would teach her to make a homemade pineapple upside-down cake. She was happy to oblige and, for Ali's birthday, Marianne thoughtfully gave Ali *The Cake Mix Doctor* by Anne Byrn, which proved to be a fabulous gift for doctoring up cake mixes.

The "We're So Proud Of You" Plate ◎ A mother of three children recently shared a special idea with me. She designed a plate that was different from her everyday china. She calls it the "You should be proud of yourself" plate, and every time her children do something she's proud of, the plate arrives at a meal. Her children started doing so many things that she had to buy three matching plates to keep up with all the accomplishments.

Family Award Night ◎ There's the Oscars and the Emmys, so why not the *Johnsons*? With the kids' help, make an award, and then duplicate it. Leave a place on the award so that you can personalize it with family members' names. Place a folder with the awards in a drawer that everyone has access to, and encourage every Sunday night (or any other night that may work for your family) as award night for celebrating each other's good deeds, kind thoughts, and positive reinforcement. You can also create family awards, and encourage each family member to prepare a paper-plate award with a special message written on it for each family member. From *The Most Thoughtful*, to *The Kindest Brother*, or *Most Helpful Sister*, awards should be presented with a story about the meaning behind the award.

Mother-Daughter Tea ◎ Surprise your daughter with a special event—high tea—at a participating hotel or restaurant. Send her an invitation to dress up, but don't tell her where you are going. She'll adore going for high tea with all the pomp and circumstance. Present something special, like a book you loved as a little girl when you were her age, or something with meaning that you can share and discuss. This teatime will become a very popular memory you both treasure.

Father-Son Night Out © The best memories are the ones shared together, so invite your son to make a wish list—not for gifts but, rather, for things he'd like to do with his dad. From fishing, to sports games, to movies, select something off the list and aim at completing the entire list over time.

Musical Chairs © Everyone has a special chair at the dinner table and it rarely changes. Have a special night of the week, or a day of the month, where everyone sits in someone else's chair. Add a memorable slant to the change of chairs by requesting that each family member pretend to be that person during dinner.

Reach For The Stars © Mike Hughes recalled a special moment he shared with his niece on a trip to Florida, while on a ferry headed to a restaurant. He commented, "We were out in the open and looking up at a magnificent star-filled sky. I pointed out to my niece how she could reach for the stars and do anything she wants to do in life. This little moment inspired her in a most meaningful way, and she wrote a paper about the experience. She was acknowledged by her teacher for how beautiful it was, and it meant so much to me that such a little thing would have such a dramatic impact on her."

The Happy Jar © Start a tradition with the happy jar, and add little slips of paper with things that make you happy each week. It's a fun thing to do, especially when children are little, and then, once the jar is filled, select a happy thought a day, and reminisce about happy times.

Sick Bell © I know a bell ringing around the clock is enough to drive anyone crazy, but giving a sick child a bell to ring when he or she is confined to bed is a really thoughtful thing to do. Set a few reasonable rules for using the bell, and then name the bell the "sick bell." While it might sound a bit old fashioned, it really works, and kids love knowing they can ring, ring, ring, and you'll come as soon as possible.

Silly Sandwiches ◎ Name-calling is fun when it comes to sandwiches. Layer up a memory by naming the sandwiches you serve at your house. From The Kitchen Sink Sandwich that has everything on it, to the Peanut Butter Surprise, which means you include something new each time—like raisins, different colored jellies and jams—or even Tuna Luna (which might be your child's favorite way to make tuna—with celery and pickles included), this name-calling activity is a fun one your kids will really enjoy, and remember throughout the years.

A Room Of Their Own ◎ One loving grandmother named Beverly Sears shared something she did for her grandchildren that proved to be the best gift of all. Beverly commented, "I transformed a room in our house for our two little grandchildren so that they'd have a room of their own when they spent the night. I wanted it to be really special and since it was a surprise, the door stayed closed until I was totally finished. I had a table and chairs for their art projects, and filled the room with toys, a colorful rug, and it was just for them. It was so successful, they couldn't wait to go to bed that first night even though it was only six o'clock in the evening!"

Anytime Coupon ◎ Give your kids a few "Anytime Coupons," which allow your child permission to interrupt you when he really needs your attention. On index cards write out a series of things the coupons are good for, ranging from "I'll read you a book anytime," to "A gigantic hug anytime." Your child can even help create the coupons. Give him one a week to use as he pleases for any time he needs some extra TLC!

Progressive Dinner ◎ This is a really fun activity to do with the kids on an evening out. Plan three locations where you'll eat dinner. Begin with salads at the first restaurant (which might be child number one's pick), and then move to the next restaurant for dinner (could be child number two's selection, perhaps hamburgers or pizza), and then onward for dessert at your local ice cream parlor.

Laugh A Day ◎ Here's a fun tradition to start at your house. Select a small toy as the family smile award. You can choose anything, from a toy from a fast food restaurant that you have lying around, to a small stuffed animal. Any family member who makes you *really* laugh gets to hold on to the keepsake. It gets passed around from member to member as the laughs mount up.

Back-And-Forth Napkin Notes ◎ Many parents love to write "I love you" notes, or "Have a great day," on napkins and hide them in a child's lunchbox. To make this little deed even more memorable, one dad told his child that every time he brings home the note, it can be traded in for a bedtime story, game they play together, or other fun activity that evening.

Boo-Boo Relief ◎ One mom created a special TLC memory for her boys, who hated using ice packs whenever they'd get hurt. She took one of their small stuffed animals from when they were babies and removed all of its filling. She created an opening at the back of the animal and, as needed, inserted an ice pack in a plastic bag inside it. Not only did it get super-cold, but it was soft on the outside, as well, and very comforting for those big boo-boos.

Build A Mountain Of Treats ◎ Tory Johnson, mother of five-year-old twins, shared this clever idea for giving gifts to kids. Since kids love opening packages, buy lots of little things, and wrap them individually in graduating boxes in a variety of colors. She stacked and tied the packages up with a colorful ribbon. This works equally wonderfully with tiny toys for kids, such as yo-yos, card games, or stickers. Or, you can fill the boxes with home-baked goodies, candy, or other treats.

Wake Up Call ◎ Any child who has been given their own clock radio, telephone, cell phone, television, or computer will tell you that's one of the most memorable gifts ever. Make the delivery memorable by having the item sitting in their room when they wake up. Add a sign to your surprise that says, "Good Morning, I'm Yours!" Or, call her on her cell phone and wake her up with a gift that will be music to her ears.

L

is for Little Things Mean A Lot

I'm frequently reminded of how the meaning of life is really captured when we celebrate the little things, and express our feelings to someone we care about. It's those minute-made memories that touch you and embrace you with kindness. It's the times when someone reaches out and says they care by showing up and doing a kind deed, or by saying the right thing at the right time, that just tells you everything will be OK. Those little things really do mean a lot, and we can never give or receive enough of them.

We've all heard the expression "it's the little things that count," and that's so true. A kiss, a hug, an "I love you," a little surprise when you were least expecting it—that's how we let someone know they are appreciated and wonderful. Those little things bond us together, and make friends feel like family, and family feel even more special. What could be more important than letting the people in your life that you care about know how much you adore them day-in and day-out?

This chapter pays tribute to all of those little things that you can do. So, even if you have little extra time but just want to be thoughtful, pick up the telephone, and let someone know you were thinking of them. Send an e-mail or a greeting card, but don't resist a thoughtful moment for one more minute!

Little Deeds And Gifts

A Sweet SOS © My friend Laurie shared how a special friend named Anne cheered her up when her mother was diagnosed with cancer. She sent Laurie a small bag containing pieces of candy. On the bag was the following:

A chocolate Kiss to remind you that you are loved!
A Tootsie Roll to remind you not to bite off more than you can chew!
A Starburst to give you a burst of energy on those days you don't have any!
Snickers to remind you to take time to laugh!
And most importantly . . . a candle to remind you that you can brighten someone else's day.

The Five-Minute Rule ◎ The five-minute rule is a great idea for every family to embrace. Simply put, the rule requires you to spend five undivided, totally attentive minutes of your time with another family member every day. Sounds easy? Try it, and you'll see what giving your undivided attention to another person really means, and the rewards that come from it.

Freezer Pleasers ◎ Is someone under the weather or feeling blue? Fill the freezer with her favorite ice cream, popsicles, or other delicious frozen treats. From totally indulgent, to sugar-free items, select favorite flavors to brighten her day.

Mail Call ◎ Send your child a letter addressed to him at home. The fun of getting mail makes your message memorable. From patting him on the back for a job well done at home, or school, be specific in your praise.

Pillow Greeting Cards ◎ Stock up on some greeting cards, and occasionally hide one of the cards under someone's pillow. From a little "I love you," to a special thank you to your kids for being so thoughtful and terrific, this good-night surprise will be especially meaningful.

Massage ◎ Give them the gift of touch with a manicure, or by cutting their nails, or by putting lotion on their hands. Bring a basket of hand-care products, or even send in a reflexologist to give them a foot massage.

Secondhand Caring ◎ When my friend Ava's mom, who is such a lovely person, was in the hospital, Ava shared what personally meant so much to her. She called it "secondhand caring," since her friends rallied around her mom, and sent little reminders and get-well wishes that were so thoughtful. One of her friends cut wildflowers from her garden, and put them in a coffee can, and left them at her door for when Ava's mom got home. Two other friends sent a nightgown, and another sent a card. That outpouring of love, Ava shared, meant more than words could say.

Write A "No Reason" Letter ◎ Here's a really lovely thing to do for a friend, family member, or even a teacher who has made a difference in your life. Write a letter of appreciation stating how he or she has made a significant difference, or state something specific they did for you that inspired you. Send the letter through the mail, and just watch how you make their day, and lift their spirits.

Be The First To Call ◎ As simple as it sounds, calling someone following a party or dinner when you've been entertained is a memorable thing to do. Call right when you get home if you are certain they are awake and still cleaning up. If you're not sure, call the next morning. When someone has a party, they hope everyone has a great time. Reassuring your friends that you had a great time gives them the gift of knowing their efforts were successful.

Make Your Presence Felt ◎ If you can't attend a very close friend's or relative's special occasion, or party, consider how you might be represented, and participate in some special way. You could send a card to arrive during the weekend, or even a good old-fashioned telegram. If the party occurs in your city, or nearby, then let your spouse or a family member drop off a small token of your affection, such as a plant, or a reminder that you regret not being present.

A Greater Waiter ◎ Next time you have a birthday party, or some special event, at a restaurant, meet with the maitre d' or waiter ahead of time, if possible. Tell him or her something about your guest of honor, and ask that the waiter comment, and wish him a happy birthday. That little extra attention can transform a mundane event, eating out, into a memorable experience.

Deliver Dinner ◎ When you know someone special has out-of-town company, or family staying with them, consider baking something, or delivering some bagels, or sweets. Whenever Hannah Brown, who was a thoughtful and remarkable lady, and adored baking, went to someone's home, she commented, "If you bring wine, they say you shouldn't have, but if you bake something special, they say thank you!"

In The Bag © When you go to a shower or party in someone's honor where gifts will be given, consider bringing half a dozen very large shopping bags to help them carry out their gifts. Transform the bags with a paper sign, taped to the bag, that says, "You shouldn't have, but I am glad you did!"

No-Delay Thank You © When you are entertained by someone and they have you over to dinner, don't hesitate to write a thank-you note, and call the next morning (not too early!), and let them know you had a fabulous time. You can also do this as you pull out of the driveway, since you know they'll be cleaning up. This no-delay thank you will really make them feel good.

E-mails To Remember © Every once in a while I get an e-mail so simple, and yet so special, I'm inspired to forward my own version to someone else. For example, recently a friend sent one that said, "Robyn—Let me count the ways I appreciate you." And then he went on to share some positive news about a project we'd been working on. It was quite refreshing after a long day to know my efforts were helpful. Your turn, now, to pass on the compliment to someone who has helped you!

A Gift For No Reason © I'm always reminded that "no reason" gifts are sometimes the nicest gifts of all. When someone gives a gift, or performs a kind deed for no reason—perhaps just to say they are thinking of you—it's really memorable. They don't expect anything in return, and the gifts are so spontaneous and timely that they always seem to take someone by surprise. Once a dear friend sent me a china angel just to let me know she was thinking of me. Another friend sent half of a birthday card on my half-birthday, which I had no earthly idea was actually happening. And a special cousin dropped off her famous mango bread, made from fresh mangoes gathered from a tree in her neighborhood, just to brighten our day. These thoughtful and meaningful gifts or deeds, given or done for no reason, are such kind-hearted gestures that we store them in our memory banks forever. Try it! You'll see what I mean when the thank-yous come pouring in.

Taking Time To Help ◎ Teacher and school office administrator, Varda Sauer, commented, "I had a student who was chronically tardy and no amount of In School Suspension seemed to teach her the lesson. I spent some time talking to her, only to find out that she did not own a clock. I bought her a clock, and she was never tardy again."

Never Too Old ◎ Star Teacher of the Year Diane Burton-Maroney shared a way she makes her students feel special and connects with them. She puts stickers that reflect their interests on homework papers that are turned in. She commented, "Even though the students are high school seniors, they actually still love the stickers. I select themes that reflect their favorite sports and hobbies, from footballs, to their favorite TV characters. We're never too old to enjoy feeling special." Diane also emphatically tells her students at the beginning of the year that she knows they're all angels and they'll break her heart if they act any other way in class. For many years, students have kept their invisible wings, and not disappointed her.

Check-Up Call ◎ Doctors make check-up calls, and so can you! Call and announce "this is a 'check-up call'" and check-up and in on someone you care about. They'll love knowing you're checking in with your "check-up call." Then really encourage a conversation that allows him or her to share what's happening. Inquire if he or she needs any advice or assistance. Life can be challenging, and we all need a listening ear and a shoulder to lean on, and this call just might do a world of good for you both.

Friends To A Tea ◎ While I was at Canyon Ranch, in Tucson, for a week, experiencing the Life Enhancement Program, I became friends with a wonderful woman named Dee, from Dallas. To say farewell as the program concluded, Dee presented me with a mug filled with packets of decaffeinated green tea (which she knew I enjoyed) and the following poem. To this day when I drink green tea, I always think of Dee and the amazing individuals I met at this life-affirming event.

When I have green tea,
I'll think of thee.
And what a remarkable gift,
You've been to me.

M

is for Most Memorable

Deeds and Gifts

Ralph Waldo Emerson said, "The only gift is a portion of thyself." When we give a gift that enters someone's heart, it becomes an indelible memory that is stored forever. Memorable deeds and gifts are priceless, and at every turn there's a moment when we have a chance to lift another person's spirit, and put a smile on their face. It is obviously not the cost of the gift or deed, but the manner in which it was given, or the sentiment behind it.

It's also ironic what we remember, and what fades from our memories. It's not the lavish gifts that always mean the most. In fact, I'll never forget the thank-you note my dad wrote me after a particular birthday party we gave for him. We had just taken him out to dinner, like we do every year, but he decided this year deserved a thank-you note. This spontaneous note was such a surprise that I have saved it for years.

The following ideas encourage memorable deeds that will always be treasured.

Ties That Bind © My dear friend Patty Brown shared a lasting memory she created as a gift to her husband. Even though Patty had never met her husband Larry's father, since he had died many years before, she wrote, "My husband's father was very present in my life, too. As his daughter-in-law, I came to know about this intelligent, very proper, gentleman through hundreds of stories and photographs, and the words of love he gave his son. I wanted to do something special for my husband, as he reminded me very much of his father. I noticed that, in each photograph, my father-in-law sported a beautiful silk hand-tied bow tie. I asked my mother-in-law if I could have the bow ties, and recall sitting on the floor sorting through a pile of these colorful creations. I contacted my framer and, together, we discussed how to most effectively frame them, finally deciding to place three bow ties in a silk-lined shadow box. The idea was a winner, so I had two more shadow boxes made for my husband's sister and brother. I then ordered three brass nameplates that stated, "The collection of Melvin A. Brown." They were placed in the shadow boxes beneath each bow tie collection, and this became a precious memory and an expression of love to a very special husband and father."

Of Days We Spent Together © When my grandparent's possessions were being divided up after they passed away, each grandchild was brought into the house to select something meaningful. I wanted something that reminded me how deeply I adored my grandparents, and I noticed a small china plate with a poem on the dining room table. I knew I had to have that plate, and that one day I'd give it to my daughter, whom I would name after my beloved Grandma Annie. The poem was titled "Friendship." Many years later, when I gave birth to a little girl, we named her Ali, and the plate sat on the table as the centerpiece at her baby naming. To this day I cherish it. The poem reads as follows:

> *Within the garden of my heart*
> *Where flowers of friendship grow*
> *There are blossoms of remembrance*
> *Forget-me-nots so blue,*
> *And purple velvet pansies*
> *To tell my thoughts of you;*
> *And roses that will always bloom*
> *Whatever be the weather*
> *Whose fragrance is the memory of*
> *Days we spent Together.*

Art From The Heart © Mike Hughes shared how, throughout the years, he's found that gifts that come from the heart are much more memorable than mundane items. A particularly memorable gift that he treasures he received from his then-eleven-year-old niece. She drew and sent him a picture of a golf green, with a flagstick, and track marks showing the ball rolling right into the hole. Topped off by a great big sun shining overhead, at the top of the page it said, "Uncle Mike #1 Golfer."

A Book Of Thanks ◎ My cousin Nancy created a special gift for her child's teacher. She helped her daughter's first grade class write a book as an end-of-the-year gift. Each child added a small part to the story, and then passed it it on to a classmate to continue it. The kids could say anything—the object was to make it funny, which the kids loved! Then she divided up the story. Each child wrote their part and illustrated it. They put it together with simple binding at a quick-copy store, and at the moving-up ceremony, on the last day, they presented her their book. They told her that, thanks to her, they could read, and even write a book. She *loved* it!"

Par For The Course ◎ Author, businessman, and speaker, Stedman Graham, shared one of the most memorable deeds that friends of his did for him. Stedman said, "I'll always remember the good deed my friend Bob Brown did for me when we went to Africa together. Prior to going, he had invited me to play golf. New to the game, little did I know that you were supposed to bring your own clubs. When we arrived in Africa, I didn't have any clubs with me, so he and the other men on the trip gave me, the guy who didn't know a thing about golf, a few clubs from each of their bags. All eight guys contributed clubs so that I would have a bag. I was really touched as each one sacrificed a few prized clubs. I'll never forget that deed, since it was really an act of kindness, and they gave of themselves in such a meaningful way."

A Time Of Caring ◎ Here's a memorable deed my Aunt Ramona's hairdresser did for her, on the birthday of her daughter, who had died ten years before. When my aunt was in his salon, he presented her with a beautiful large-faced watch, and said, "I know this is a particularly difficult time for you." My aunt adores large-faced watches, and Phillip searched to find the perfect watch for her, one that he knew she'd love. My aunt commented, "August 2nd continues to be an extremely difficult day, even though Mona passed away ten years ago. This kind deed touched my heart more than he'll ever know, and really meant a lot to me."

That Special Dressing © Harriette Bawarsky gives a memorable gift when she goes to her friends' homes for dinner. She brings a special balsamic vinaigrette salad dressing that she calls her "secret formula," and everyone adores it. For a clever presentation, she washes out an empty wine bottle, and then refills it with this special memorable dressing. Next, she puts the cork back to seal it, and wraps it up with a seasonal dishcloth in a pretty color and theme matching the occasion. She places the dressing in the center of a cloth, pulls up the sides, and ties a raffia string around the neck of the bottle to hold it in place. She then adds a special hang-tag which guarantees a bottomless lifetime refill.

A Change Of Your Dress! © Create a really fun, funky address book. Purchase an address book, and pass it around so that your gift recipients' friends and family can enter their addresses, telephone numbers, cell numbers, e-mails, etc. Then collage it with paper and magazine clippings to make a new front cover, and apply clear packaging tape to the work you've done. Whenever you have a chance to update someone's address book, it's a memorable deed that really is appreciated.

SOS For Forgetfulness? © If you know someone who is commonly forgetting things, here's a meaningful gift you can create for them. Take a calendar and place a photograph of each person they know on their particular birthday or anniversary. It will make remembering those special dates easier. Also, make a VIP telephone list, with the really important numbers enlarged and highlighted on the list.

Safe And Sound © The most meaningful gift you can give your family is to be the "smoke detector safety guru." Research the best safety practices, and share them with family members. Here are a few favorites to know:

- Check your smoke detector.
- Purchase a carbon monoxide detector.
- Check how flammable and poisonous items are stored. Are your paint cans and other items in a safe place?

• Are there any mats, or rugs, not secured, where someone could easily fall?

Bring In The Clowns ⓒ A most memorable party caterer, Tony Conway of Legendary Events, planned a birthday party for an eight-year-old girl who was dying of cancer. He told me that, "We actually had the party on the grounds of the Children's Hospital. She had always dreamed of being in the circus, so we brought the circus to her with some help from the Ringling Bros. and Barnum & Bailey Circus group, and their clown school in Florida. All the children from the hospital that could attend were invited, along with this special child's family and friends. It was magical, and has always had the most special place in my heart."

Now And Then ⓒ Give a photograph of a family member then and now in the same frame. Find a double-sided picture frame, and put their baby photo or a favorite picture from childhood on one side, and a current photograph on the other side.

Send It Ahead ⓒ Next time you're invited to someone's house for dinner, find out what their color scheme is and send flowers ahead. Inform them they are coming and, the day before the party, have the flowers delivered. If you don't know exactly what type of flowers the host prefers, then send a beautiful orchid in a pretty pot.

Scrap Book To Treasure ⓒ My friend Shirley is incredible at helping us all preserve memories, and shows up at every special occasion with a scrapbook she has compiled, allowing everyone to add their sentiments, or good wishes. To commemorate a special project her parents had worked on (which was a fundraiser for the new Holocaust Museum in Montreal), and in honor of all their hard work, for over a year she took every photograph she had of her grandparents and parents and made copies of them, placing them in chronological order with little captions beneath each one. In addition, she wrote her parents an eight-page summary of all the stories and anecdotes her grandparents and parents had told her, and also asked my three kids to write their grandparents a letter including every memory they had of their great-grandparents. The book meant so much to Shirley's parents that her mother has taken that scrapbook to every meeting for the museum.

It's A Snap ⓒ Carry a single-use camera with you in your car or purse, and you'll be so surprised how many special memories you can capture. You will be able to catch so many moments in time, and then surprise the subjects with a picture. Save them in a file for future gifts to frame.

Give A Just In Case Gift ⓒ Manicurist Faye Ivanova remembers a favorite deed that her client Sandy Abrams did for her. "Sandy had picked up chicken soup for someone who wasn't feeling well, but what made her gesture so memorable was that she brought the rest of us a cup of soup as well, to put away for a rainy day. It was just so kind to worry and think about us, just in case."

Give A Day In The Life ⓒ Talk about a day to remember! Do you know someone who has always wanted to work at a TV station, be a disc jockey, doctor, lawyer, politician, or perhaps a rocket scientist? Go to work and arrange for them to spend a day shadowing someone in that field. It could be a well-known person in your community, or someone you know through a friend. This might take some serious connections and persistence, but with a little work, you can pull it off, and it will be one of the most memorable days they've ever had.

Newly Divorced? ⓒ Have a girlfriend who has recently gotten divorced? Give her a colorful bag filled with her favorite brand of shampoo, or a set of new towels (with her new initials if she took back her maiden name), and add a note that says, "You need to wash that man right out of your hair! We're 'hair' if you need us!"

A Book On Tape ⓒ Knowing that her best friend Marla had just suffered the loss of both parents, Tracy Green did a memorable deed that Marla said touched her beyond words. Tracy sent a note with the audiocassette of *When Bad Things Happen To Good People* by Rabbi Harold S. Kushner. The book on tape was perfect for those tough times alone, especially when you have time to think while driving. Marla said that the tape provides a reassuring and inspiring message that continues to help her.

A Stranger With Heart ⓒ When Marci Spatz was a young girl, only thirteen years old, and visiting the theater district on Broadway to see a play, she dined at a restaurant before the play. At dinner, she realized her solid gold watch, one that her beloved grandfather had given her, had fallen off her arm. She was hysterical, and caused such a scene crying that a gentleman asked what was wrong, and inquired about the details of the watch. She told him the style of the watch and, within minutes, he disappeared into the crowd. To Marci's shock and amazement, the gentleman arrived an hour later with a look-alike watch that was the same exact style as the one Marci lost. It was a new watch, but resembled her old one. Marci's mother said she couldn't accept it, but the man insisted. It turned out he was a wealthy hotelier from Las Vegas who just wanted to do a good deed. The restaurant vouched for his kindness and, to this day, Marci has loved that watch and never forgot his magnanimous deed.

The Present Of Your Presence © When giving a gift to someone from a group of friends or family members, invite everyone who gave the gift to also help present it. While it takes a little organizing, this special delivery from the entire group will be a present that has major presence!

Memorable Gift Wraps & Deliveries

To make your gift extra special, consider the gift wrap and deliver it with pizzazz. Here are some gift-wrapping tips to get you started:

Top Off Your Gift With Pizzazz. Add a present topper to the gift that matches the theme. Attach to the bow or ribbon a brightly colored hairbrush and hair bows for a teenager, or luggage tags for a travel-related gift. Or, select cooking utensils and spatulas for a bridal shower, or pacifiers to welcome a new baby. Your gift will scream, "You're special" the second they see it!

Give A Gift In A Gift. When giving a purse, be sure to include a pretty hand mirror, or a gift certificate, or pre-paid gift card to a favorite store. Put a gift card that can be used at the store inside a DVD or CD for an instant hit, or hang a diamond necklace on a teddy bear, or doll.

Wrap Your Gift In Something Unpredictable. Wrap up a cookbook in a colander, slip that diamond ring on the thornless stems of long-stemmed roses in the florist box, or use a bandana or colorful cloth napkin tied off with a ribbon for an instant wrap for a bottle of wine.

Don't Forget The Surprise Delivery! Tie a string to your gift and unravel it all over the house. They'll wake up to it in the morning. Or, place the gift in the seat of her car, or even leave it on his nightstand in the middle of the night. From the refrigerator, to inside her book bag, the element of surprise enhances your gift.

The manner of giving is worth more than the gift.

—Corneille, seventeenth-century playwright

N

is for New Baby

Talk about memories! Nine months, and waiting for the big moment. When a baby is on his or her way, there are endless details, and things to do. The birth of a baby is one of the most memorable occasions for parents, siblings, and the entire family. When our children were born, I thought of every imaginable way to commemorate their births. I created endless keepsakes that went far beyond the traditional scrapbooks. It was all so exciting and now, many years later, I'm so grateful. From saving what our son wore on the ride home from the hospital, so that his little sister, six years later, could also travel home in it, to preserving and framing our daughter's first dress, to saving their favorite toys, I've gone to great lengths to transform these items into treasured memories from their childhoods.

This chapter features a vast selection of creative ideas that will help you make your bundle of joy's birth, or the arrival of someone you adore's baby, really memorable. From birth announcements, to baby showers and gifts for both mom and baby, it's so easy to make things memorable when a baby is born, and your deeds and thoughtful actions will be truly welcomed. Not only will you create a memory that will be lasting, it will mean so much to those very busy new parents who only need a good night's sleep!

Birth Announcements

Baby's Breath ☺ Purchase seed packages of baby's breath and print your birth announcement on a sticker. Add it to the back of the package, or print it on a piece of paper, and glue it on permanently. Add the message, "Our news is breathtaking! Edie and Billy Brown announce the birth of a baby girl! Annie Lauren, November 2, 1986."

A Home-run Hit ◎ When Julie and George gave birth to the baby boy they had long hoped for, they created a fabulous birth announcement for their son's arrival. They purchased dozens of official baseballs with red stitching, and imprinted them with their new baby boy's stats, including his name, birth date, weight, and length. Packaged in a colorful box, these baseball baby announcements were sent to family and friends announcing the baby slugger.

Twins ◎

Double the diapers,
Double the fun,
We gave birth to twins,
Instead of just one!

Paper Dolls ◎ Draw a series of paper dolls from dotted lines on a long piece of a paper and write your birth announcement information with a statistic on each doll. Print the baby's date of birth, weight, and length. For a creative touch, include a pair of children's scissors for paper dolls they can actually cut out.

Message In A Baby Bottle ◎ Like a message in a bottle, send a baby bottle with the announcement rolled and tucked neatly inside. Tie a pink or blue bow around the neck of the bottle for a special touch. This also makes a cute baby-naming favor if you add baby's photo, and confetti in pink or blue.

Nursery Rhyme ◎ When a couple is hoping for a specific sex, and he or she arrives . . . here's a fun way to announce it. On the birth announcement put a clock and the time the baby was born with this line:

Hickory Dickory Dock,
The _____'s are all in shock!
Our nursery is finally complete,
Baby _____ accomplished our feat!

Diaper Pin And Paper ◎ Use either homemade or store-bought birth announcements, and add a diaper pin in the corner on an angle, or centered across the top, for a memorable touch. You can spruce up ordinary invitations with these special additions and, if you want to go one step further, place a small photo of your newborn on the pin and attach it to the birth announcement.

Gifts For The New Mom And Dad

A Countdown Scrapbook © Here is a fabulous way to give the new mom and dad a gift that will be treasured forever. When the couple announces they are going to have a baby, congratulate them with two single-use cameras wrapped in a pretty box. Include a stack of signs you make on heavyweight paper that begin with the month she tells you and continue with "Month Two," "Month Three," "Month Four," "Month Five," and so on. Encourage them to take pictures as they prepare for baby's arrival, from picking out the furniture and getting the room ready, to mom's favorite (and least favorite) foods while pregnant. Call with monthly reminders to keep them on track saving memories. Once it's time for the big day, request the cameras be returned. Develop the pictures and create a pregnancy scrapbook filled with newspaper headlines you've saved monthly, and other world events and fun things that have occurred during the time period.

A Vice Kit © Did she give up coffee, diet sodas, or chocolate? When she's able to indulge, give the proud parents a gift that gives them the green light for fun. Grab a basket, and fill it up with things the couple couldn't enjoy during the pregnancy. Include champagne, wine, gourmet (fully caffeinated) coffee, decadent chocolates, a gift certificate for a local sushi restaurant, and just about anything else that will make the appreciative new parents remember a little of pre-baby life.

Hers And Hers. © Here's a gift for mom and her baby girl! Matching bracelets are the sterling choice. Give the new mom a silver (or gold) bracelet, with the baby's name and birth date engraved inside, and give baby a sterling silver bracelet with the matching information. For a boy, give a his-and-his set of cufflinks, or a money clip with the same.

Petals Of Love ⓒ When our daughter, Ali, was born, the pink floral arrangements were so beautiful that I didn't want to part with them as they began to wilt. To preserve the flowers, I placed the bouquets hanging upside down so that the petals didn't touch each other, and kept them out of direct sunlight. A few weeks later, I put the dried flowers into a jar, and sealed it. Sixteen years later, to my surprise, the petals, while faded over time, are still a special reminder of how tickled pink we were upon Ali's arrival.

Baby Gifts

A Quilt Of Love ⓒ When I was one year old, my mother had a photograph taken of me in a pretty mint green cotton dress. You can only imagine how surprised I was at the age of thirty-something to find the dress from the photograph sitting on my mom's nightstand, tucked away in a storage box. Inspired by the dress, when our daughter Ali was born, I had her photographed in her first party dress, and saved it, too. When it was time to decorate Ali's room, I framed both of the dresses under glass in shadow boxes to preserve them. The dresses, hanging side by side, encouraged the theme of her room, which ultimately became a collage of memorable moments sewn into a quilt, pillows, and a wall hanging. Each item was made from her baby clothes that I had saved combined with adorable appliqués, monograms, and my grandmother's and mother's monogrammed handkerchiefs. With the help of a seamstress experienced in quilting, we pieced it together into a beautiful design. I also had some of the fabrics embroidered with "I love you" in French and English, as well as Ali's first doll's dress, baby socks, and bows she wore in her hair. From birthday dresses sewn to pillows, to a wall hanging with the left-over pieces, the entire room became a lasting memory Ali will treasure forever!

Bonnet To Bouquet ⓒ When Alison Peppers was born, her mother, Angela, received a beautiful white linen baby bonnet from a friend. It was made from a hankie, with two ribbons for tying, and a stitch at two corners so that it could be worn on baby's head. A special poem was included that shared how to transform the baby bonnet into a wedding keepsake hankie that Alison would one day carry down the aisle, wrapped around her bouquet. Alison's wedding was this year and the bonnet was transformed with the snip of a pair of scissors. Her mother shared with me the poem that accompanied this lovely gift:

I'm just a little hankie,
As square as square can be.
But with a stitch or two,
They'll make a bonnet out of me.

I'll be worn home from the hospital
Or on a special day,
Then I'll be carefully pressed
And neatly packed away.

For her wedding we've been told
Every well-dressed bride must have that something old,
So what could be more fitting than to find little me?
A few stitches snipped and a wedding hankie I will be.

And if per chance it is a boy,
Some day he'll surely wed.
So to his bride he can present the hankie,
Once worn upon his head.

A Prized Possession © Tory Johnson shared a really memorable gift that she loves to give special friends upon the birth of a baby. It is an antique sterling silver trophy cup engraved with the baby's name and birth date. Tory arranges beautiful fresh flowers inside the trophy, and sends a note to the new parents with her prize-winning gift that says, "Your baby is already a winner with parents like you." For a special Mother's Day surprise, she gave her close friend, talk show host Kelly Ripa, a gorgeous sterling silver English trophy from the 1800s. She had spent weeks searching for it and, upon finding it, had the names and birth dates of Kelly and her husband Mark Consuelos's three children engraved on it. You can also use a new trophy, which is very reasonable if you don't want to purchase a sterling silver version, but this is one gift that will become a prized possession.

Stuffed With Love © Often a child will bond with one special stuffed animal, toy, or blanket, and it becomes a treasured item. Before that toy becomes threadbare, or worn to a frazzle, commemorate it with a framed photograph. That photograph of your child's favorite friend will become a time-treasured memory over the years.

The First Precious Days Of Life ◎ Lorie Lewis shared a memorable experience she had when her first child was born. She recounts, "When I was in the hospital, after my baby was born, a very dear friend came to take pictures. A few days later, they presented me with a photo album containing those first pictures, and the front page of the newspaper from the day he was born, along with his horoscope, and a few other clippings. I still look at the book with great appreciation." Other items you could include are a canceled stamp with the date, the week's memorable magazines, and even a video of the nightly news.

And The Gift Goes On ◎ One of the most memorable gifts ever was given from one sister to another. Since Laurie was an avid scrapbooker, when her sister's baby was born she created a scrapbook filled with snapshots she took at the hospital and baby naming. She included loads of details that she caught while the parents were busy taking care of baby. But, the amazing part of this gift was how she offered to continue it through the years. Here's what the card said, and you'll see what I mean:

Precious photographs and memories fill this book,
Over the years you'll take many a look
As the memories grow, your gift will, too,
Just supply me the pictures and I'll preserve them for you!

A Song For Justin ◎ When our son, Justin, was born (he is now twenty-three years old), I wrote a song for him. It was elementary, at best, but I wrote the music and the lyrics, and put it in his baby book. While it never made the top ten list, it certainly ranked at the top of his list, when he heard it years later, as an adult.

What's Up Doc? ◎ Here's a really unique gift that Jack Morton gives for new arrivals: he has a baby pillow monogrammed with the baby's name, birth date, weight and length, and the name of the doctor who delivered him, or her. To make this gift more creative, add the front page of the newspaper on the day the baby was born, or build a theme around sleep time, and include a lullaby tape, book, and stuffed animal.

A Reader's Dozen © Help the new parents along with a dozen books for the first year of baby's life. Choose *Goodnight Moon, Pat the Bunny*, and other classics. Include a book for mom and dad in the line-up of must-reads as well, and order a pair of bookends with baby's name and birthday. You can also paint it yourself if you are artistic. Or, include a nightlight, lamp for baby's room, and some personalized sleepers matching the themes of the books.

Zoo–m In On The Baby © If that baby has everything, give a gift to the local zoo in honor of baby . . . perhaps naming a baby animal in your new arrival's honor. Give baby a stuffed version of his/her real animal, a picture of the baby animal with a card describing the animal, and your contribution in his/her honor. Be sure to include a promise for a trip to the zoo when he or she is ready!

First Things First © Consider giving a baby who is born prior to a holiday a special gift. Depending on the family's religion, have a color-ful bib monogramed with the baby's name and the occasions such as: _____'s first Easter, Passover, Christmas, Chanukah, or any of the holi-days the family will soon be celebrating.

We can do no great things.

Only small things with great love.

—Mother Teresa

is for Office Parties and Career-Related Gifts

Office parties—gifts for your co-workers and the boss who has everything! For most individuals, those are scary thoughts. How do you entertain hundreds of employees while pleasing a variety of ages, tastes, and interests? Or, how do you find the perfect gift for the boss who is hard to please, or that co-worker who has been so supportive of you and to whom you wish to say thanks, but in an appropriate way?

The key to an office party, big or small, is to provide something that the group values. The same goes for giving a fellow employee or your boss a gift. If your office is filled with health-food fanatics, then avoid dessert parties. Low-cal smoothies, or yogurt breaks, are in order. The key to being memorable is to be creative, and that doesn't mean you have to spend loads of money. Think about your employees' interests, talents, likes and dislikes, and get them involved to work as a team when party planning, and gift giving.

When planning a successful office party, it takes a great deal of time and preparation. Having overseen parties for thousands of people in my party-planning days, I know firsthand what it takes to pull off the party of the century. It begins with a memorable theme, detailed planning, loads of hours, and precise execution. And then, when giving gifts, it's important to know something more about your co-worker or boss than what he eats for lunch every day.

This chapter will help you throw a memorable party and be a gifted giver throughout the year. For additional party ideas that are also appropriate for your office, see "P is for Parties," and for additional gift ideas refer to those specific sections.

Office Parties

Dance Fever © A law firm threw one of the most indulgent office parties I've ever heard about—they took their entire office plus spouses, via a chartered bus, to a gourmet dinner at a major resort. The company hired a band and had two professional dancers give tango lessons. They served a fabulous dinner and danced the night away.

Day Off © Let your office take a vote and decide what they want to do this year for their holiday party. Give the employees a choice between an employee party or a day off. Guess which one will win?

Have A Mickey Mouse Party © This is a fun way to celebrate a little time off. Close the office an hour early for no reason, and bring in snacks and desserts. In the tradition of Mickey Mouse: "M–I–C–K–E–Y . . . Why? Because we love you!"

Compute This Invite! © If time allows, and you want to be totally memorable, program a screen saver that's an invitation to your big holiday office party on each employee's computer. This is easier to do if you have a small office, but if you have a larger office you can post it at a central computer and position the monitor so that all your employees can view it when they arrive at work.

The Founding Father © One company held an event that was quite meaningful to both the family that owned the company and the employees: they celebrated the founder of the company's 100th birthday and had a birthday party in his memory. They had a tribute to the founding father who had the vision and began the company.

Do Something Fun Day © When kids are out of school for a national holiday, but your office isn't closed, instead of a party, consider giving employees an afternoon off, and call it a "do something fun with your family" day. Provide half-off coupons (or passes) to the local amusement park, and give employees notice ahead of time to line up their kids, and encourage a family fun day.

Wear Something Silly Day ☺ To boost employee morale, invite them to wear something silly, or a favorite clothing item they saved from their youth. Employees will arrive at work in the most amazing costumes and be the talk of the water cooler. Award the employees with the silliest outfits a super-silly prize.

Gifts And Deeds At Work

For The World's Best Boss ☺ Let your boss know you appreciate him or her by collaborating with everyone in the office on a group gift. The key is to learn something special about them that reflects their interests outside of the office. Are they a gardener, a golfer, a runner, a swimmer? Find out something about them that shows a reflection of their tastes and you'll be more memorable. If you're not sure what to get him or her, think small—mini-televisions, mp3 players, tiny cameras, and anything that fits in the palm of your hand, is portable, and state-of-the-art.

Gifts That Keep On Giving ☺ Tony Conway commented, "The two most memorable gifts I have ever gotten were given to me by a group of friends. The first was when an animal was adopted in my name to support the zoo (they knew I am a total animal lover), and the other was when a group of six wonderful clients got together and planted six trees in Atlanta in my name for my birthday. I love saying today that they are thriving and living well in Piedmont Park where they were planted!"

VIP Parks Here ☺ One office rewarded their in-house self-proclaimed party planner, who went to great lengths every holiday (and birthday, new baby, etc.), with a VIP (Very Important Party Planner) parking space close to the front door of the office. She worked overtime, and gave it her all, asking for nothing in return.

It's In The Cards ☺ If you have a boss who is a bit disorganized, or absolutely loves being organized, put together a card file in a handsome leather holder with all of his VIP clients' business cards. This takes a bit of time to pull off as you collect the cards. As an alternative you can make copies of cards. This is a really thoughtful gift for him to keep in his desk drawer, briefcase, or car, especially in case of an electrical power outage, or unexpected computer glitch. This way, his crucial numbers and contacts are at his fingertips.

In The News ◎ Whenever you spot a business article that's positive and memorable about a company you wish to acknowledge during the holidays, cut out the article and save it in a special place. As the holiday season approaches, include the clipping in your greeting card, and write a note that says, "It was a very good year! We're proud to know you."

Author Author ◎ Do a search on one of the popular search engines on the web and print out all the positive reviews you can find listed on an author's books. Arrange them in the order of the years the books were published and design a cover that's very creative. Have the copy bound at a quick-copy store.

Attorney Privileges ◎ Give your favorite lawyer a gift he or she will remember forever. Fill to the brim an inexpensive briefcase with sweets and snacks. Add a note that says, "I'll be brief. You're my favorite lawyer on earth!" Then be sure to brief him on how much he means to you no matter what you give, even if it's a letter or card thanking him.

Superhero ◎ An attorney often does the work of a superhero, so check out the toy store to express your gratitude, and search for a superhero toy to say "thank you." One appreciative client did just that, and to thank his attorney went to the toy store and purchased a battery-operated talking Darth Vader. At the push of a button it said, "May the force be with you." To this day, it's still one of the lawyer's favorite gifts, and sits on his office desk to remind him to fight off evil.

What's Up Doc? ◎ Doctors all have special preferences—from fine wines to favorite foods—so find out what they like to make your gifts memorable. If your doctor's a coffee drinker, give a gift card to his favorite coffeehouse. Or, give him a magazine subscription that reflects his interests, so that he can put it in his waiting room after he enjoys it. Or, find out his favorite restaurant and give him a gift certificate there. The key with doctors (and any professional) is to do some homework first.

Teacher's Pet ⊚ If your teacher has a (real) pet, then give a gift that caters to the pet. That's right! Put together a doggie bag of treats for the pet, a new leash or collar, or some special accessory her pet will enjoy. For example, pet bowls come in all shapes and sizes, including clever themes that are very decorative. Search for a bowl, like one mom did, and then add a special note. She actually located a dog bowl in the shape of a crown and added the note, "Thanks for treating our daughter royally!"

A Lesson Plan For Gift Giving ⊚ Need help with what to give your child's teacher? Plan ahead of time and take notes. Observe (or have your child report) details to you he or she notices. Does the teacher always wear pretty pins on her jacket, have pierced ears, or have a glass collection of paperweights on his desk? Keep notes and customize your gift to fit his or her interests. One year I gave a teacher an angel for her angel collection. Another time, I selected a pretty pin since I noticed that she loved accessories. If you are at a total loss for what to give, purchase a tote bag and have the teacher's initials or name put on it. Fill it with sweet or savory snacks, or fresh fruit, for a snack attack!

Teacher Creatures Of Comfort ⊚ Think of those foods that comfort us all, from soups to hot chocolate, apple cider to comfort foods of all sorts. From packaged macaroni and cheese, to popcorn and sodas, be creative. Fill a bag or basket with these creature comforts for your favorite teacher, and add a note, "Thank you for making my child feel so comfortable this year. Enjoy these teacher creature comforts on us!"

Meant To Be! ⊚ If you have a teacher who was meant for your child, tell her so by filling up a container with packaged mints of all descriptions. Add a few LifeSavers as well, and then attach a note that says, "As teachers go, you were 'mint' for us!"

To Your Sweet Success ⊚ Everyone loves receiving sweets in the mail, and food products make for great business gifts. One holiday season, Tory Johnson sent each of her clients a wonderful thank-you and a gorgeous barrel of chocolate-covered gourmet pretzels with a note saying, "Women For Hire wishes you *sweet success* in the New Year."

A Memorable Idea At Work © One gentleman shared his favorite gift with me, one that he gives himself daily while at work. He asks himself every morning when he arrives, "What's the one thing I've avoided doing?" Then, he does it. He said that one question is the best gift ever, since he's accomplished so much at work and in his life by not postponing things, or procrastinating.

Retirement Day © In 2001, when my dad, approaching retirement, decided to move and consolidate his office, I visited him at the old office. What touched me most was that he had saved numerous inspiring poems and notes that he wished to share with his staff and pinned them to his bulletin board. I asked his office manager to make me a copy of those papers, and they have become a treasure I enjoy reading from time to time. I gave an excerpt from one of the poems back to my dad, as a tribute written on a plaque, to remind him how I appreciate and respect his work ethic. Here's the poem that he had posted:

Good Business

The reason people pass one door . . .
To patronize another store,
Is not because the busier place . . .
Has better silks, or gloves, or lace.
Or special prices, but it lies . . .
In pleasant words and smiling eyes;
The only difference, I believe,
Is in the treatment folks receive.

—Edgar A. Guest

Retired But Admired © If you are coordinating a group gift for a retiring boss or co-worker, ask everyone to write a letter stating his or her favorite thing about them. Place all the letters in a handsome leather box, or a pretty mirrored or fabric-covered one for a woman. Have a self-sticking brass plate engraved with his or her name, date of retirement, and the phrase, *"You might be retired, But you'll forever be admired!"* Attach it to the box for a memorable keepsake.

Overdo It © If someone you know is retiring, give a gift in excess, and overdo it. For example, if he's a golfer, give him a year's worth of golf balls with a note, "Wishing you greener pastures ahead." How about a year's supply of suntan lotion for someone headed to the beach, or massages and spa services for a year, or a membership to an athletic club? Whatever the gift is, overdo it, and you're sure to get your point across.

> You cannot do a kindness too soon,
> for you never know how soon it will be too late.
> —Ralph Waldo Emerson

$\mathcal{P}$
is for Parties With Panache

It's Party Time! Everyone loves a great party, and the secret to a party's success is to make the guests feel at home, and entertain them beyond belief. When giving a party, everyone wants to make it memorable, but, often, even the most lavish parties miss the moment. Parties that are successful make the guests feel comfortable and welcomed, but they also provide a few hours delight for the senses with memorable food, fun, and festivities.

This chapter presents a wide range of choices for your party's theme. Whether you're throwing a party for kids or adults, instead of throwing your hands up and endlessly worrying, just take care of the details and add pizzazz to your party. Do your homework, plan and consider all the little things that will make your party the most memorable one ever, and pour on the creativity. Here are some super suggestions for creating a party with panache.

Suggested Themes

The key to a memorable party is the theme and how you carry it out. Here's a list inspired by Let's Celebrate, a special events company:

A Kid Again
A Taste Of The South
    (North, Atlanta, Chicago,
    New York, etc.)
American Salute

Arabian Night
Army Party
Around The World
Art Deco Ball (Masque Ball)
Balloon Fantasy

Beach Party
Bright Lights
Broadway
Cabaret
Candy Land
Country-Western Jamboree
Cruise Ship
Carnival
Casino
Celestial
Come As You Were
Construction Site Party
Dance Fever
Denims and Diamonds
Desert Theme
Dessert Party
Diner Theme
Dinosaur Madness
Diploma Celebration
Disco
Diva Party
Election Night USA
Enchanted Forest
40s, 50s, 60s, 70s (etc.)
Fairy Tale
Fiesta
Fifties Frolic
Florida's Flamingo Road
Futuristic
Garden Party
Girl's Night Out
Glamour Gal
Golf Festival
Hawaiian Luau
Haunted Happenings
Hip-Hop Rock 'n' Roll
Hollywood
It's a Small World

Jazz Brunch
Las Vegas
Magic
Mardi Gras
Mexican Fiesta
Movie Madness
Murder Mystery
Musical Instruments
Modern-Day Music
New York, New York
New Year's Eve Celebration
Olympic Games
Oktoberfest
Pirates
Putting On the Ritz
Phantom of the Opera
Prom Night
Race Car
Renaissance Fair
Recovery Room
Safari Adventures
Seaside
Seaport Seascape
Secret Garden
Shopping, Hats, Shoes, etc.
Songs
Southern Delight
South Pacific
Space
Sports Cars
Sporting Event
States
Stock Market
Story Book
Super Heroes
Super Bowl Madness
Surfing
Survivor

Sweet Delights	TV Classics
Tacky Party	Under the Sea
Time Tunnel	Wild, Wild West
Toys	Winter Wonderland
Treasure Hunt	World Series
Tropical Paradise	

Be Creative With Your Party Location

One way to add a memorable flair to your birthday party, wedding, or special event is the location you select at which to have it. Here are some memorable choices:

* An Historic Home or Private Estate
* Art Gallery or Museum (the more original the type of museum, the better)
* Private Dining Room at a Swanky Restaurant
* Botanical Garden or Special Garden
* Winery
* Spa or Athletic Club
* Rooftop Plaza
* Ice Cream Parlor

Best Kid's Parties Ever

I'm A Little Teapot Party © A tea party is ideal for little girls who love to dress up and pretend. Glue tea bags on the invitations for a tea-riffic touch. Serve teacakes, warm cider, or flavored caffeine-free teas, and add lots of fuss. Start off the birthday girl with a collection of pretty teacups and saucers at this party. Every year on her birthday, add a new teacup. Fun activities could include playing "pin the teacup on the saucer," or having a Mother Goose–like character (mom or grandma dressed up to the hilt) reading a few favorite stories. They could have everyone recite and act out the nursery rhyme "I'm A Little Teapot"!

Get Goofy Party © A goofy party is one of the most memorable, since everything at this party is simply goofy. Serve dessert first, and then lunch, and be as silly as possible. Serve English muffins with smiling faces made from pizza ingredients and olives, play super-goofy games like "pin the legs on the octopus," and make sure the requested dress is backwards and totally mismatched clothing! To make the party even goofier, place a sticker of a famous cartoon character, or another celebrity that appeals to kids, on each guest's back, and challenge every guest to see who they have on their backs from clues they exchange.

Cookie Party © Calling all smart cookies to a cookie baking, making, and decorating party! It's fun to let a small group of kids roll out the dough and then have an adult do the baking—but while the cookies are baking, have animal crackers and other pre-baked cookies ready to frost. Offer the kids an assortment of frostings and candy toppings, and have Popsicle sticks handy to do the spreading. Instant decorating offers a fun treat that can be gobbled up.

Dino—Mite Party © Bakery owner Ryan McEntyre commented on one of the best birthday parties he'd seen. Ryan said, "An outstanding birthday party one little boy had was created around a dinosaur/caveman theme. Everyone was invited to dress up like a caveman or cavewoman and all of the food was dino-themed. The cake was in the shape of a Tyrannosaurus Rex, there were Pterodactyl Wings (hot wings), Stegosaurus Bites (celery), Bug Juice (red punch), and all sorts of pick-up foods that were dinosaur-related. Party games included 'pin the tail on the dinosaur' and a version of caveman hide-and-seek."

An Art—rageous Party © To have an art party, purchase an inexpensive plastic chair for each child. (They are readily available at toy and dime stores.) Provide stickers and alphabet letters and have each child decorate their chair. Since they'll dry instantly, use the chairs to play musical chairs, and let each child take their work of art home.

Paint The Room Party © When Artist Maggie Hasbrouck was knocking out a wall in her studio, she decided to first have a paint-the-wall party for her daughter Jane's third birthday. It was the most memorable party ever as all the children had a blast actually painting on the walls of the room.

Star Struck © One of the most memorable parties we had for our daughter Ali was when she was three. It was a "Star Struck" party. Guests were invited to dress as movie stars and, of course, the parents had the best time helping their little celebrities get star-studded. The birthday cake was in the shape of a star, with Ali's photograph on top, and star wands and star-shaped lollipops were the favors.

Pancake Party © A fun party to have for a birthday girl or boy is a pancake breakfast party. Have each stack of pancakes served with whipped cream on top and place a selection of toppings on the table to decorate the pancakes with silly faces. Take a photograph of each child with their pancake portrait, and then eat up all the creative designs. Place birthday candles in chocolate chip pancakes for dessert, and serve ice cream scoops on top of—you guessed it—more pancakes!

Theme Supreme © Sheri Hardin is well known for the birthday bashes she throws for her kids. Each party is based on a unique theme and is nothing short of fabulous. For seven-year-old Sage's birthday, she created an army theme. Invitations mimicked an actual 1931 telegram Sage's grandfather had received and saved. They changed the words to include the party details, and it read, "You are hereby requested to report for duty (and lots of fun) to celebrate Sage Hardin's seventh birthday." Civilian time was given, and the RSVP was to Sergeant Sheri. As Sage's friends arrived, army attire and all the trimmings greeted them, including a full-blown backyard obstacle course Sage's dad, Bo, had constructed. Camouflaged lunchboxes and personalized dog tags with their names (done inexpensively at an army supply store) were the party favors. A birthday cake in the shape of a tank was the centerpiece. For their girls' parties, an invitation shaped like a credit card with the party information on it was sent inviting shoppers to a Shopping Scavenger Hunt at the mall. (Be sure to get permission first with mall officials for this one.) Chaperones were assigned to each group, and it was such a hit that they repeated it for each daughter's birthday. Groups were challenged to see how much money they could save from a designated amount as they were confronted with clues, and had one hour to find the treasures, and bring them back. The girls had to find something to buy for a dime, and got points for collecting movie ticket stubs, purchasing one of the books they were reading in school, posing for instant photographs taken in front of specific stores described by the clues, and more. Points were earned for each mission accomplished and totaled while they had cake and ice cream at the mall. Everyone was a winner, and each guest received a shopping bag purse filled with shopping essentials, like gum, lip-gloss, and candy cell phones.

Get Fit Party © Get fit to party, that is! An exercise party was ideal for a group of energetic five-year-olds. Guests were invited to come dressed to work out and an exercise dance routine was taught and led by a certified exercise instructor at her studio. An obstacle course was set up so that each child could test their skill and, after forty-five minutes of fun and intense activity, the tired crew was happy to exercise their jaws with ice cream and cake.

A Dandy Candy Hunt © Don't save a hunt just for Easter—this is a party idea that works year-round for children ages two and up. Decorate the backyard with wrapped candy that's safe for the age you are entertaining and have the kids go on a candy treasure hunt. Sprinkle the candy, and also stickers and toys, balls, and other fun things that they'll enjoy, all over the yard. Begin the party by instructing each child to decorate their bag with stickers and markers.

Kiddie Parade © A parade of any sort is always fun, especially when the kids make their costumes from paper bags. Cut the head and arm holes out and allow each child to transform their brown paper bag into a fabulous, colorful creation. Supply stickers, paint, feathers, glitter, and the works, and encourage each child to create a costume for the parade. Then hand out tambourines and noisemakers for a pint-sized parade around the backyard or inside a gym or auditorium.

Nursery Rhyme Time © Have a nursery-rhyme party for young children and invite everyone to come dressed as their favorite character. Make all the activities fit nursery rhymes from playing "Pin the smile back on Humpty Dumpty" to "Decorating Jack and Jill's pail" with markers and stickers. The pail can hold the candy you'll get to take home as your party favor. The cake can be your child's favorite nursery rhyme brought to life.

Think Pink ⊚ My childhood friend Linda Reisman threw an especially cute party and decorated everything in pink. She used pink tablecloths, napkins, cups, silverware, pink flowers in pink water (thanks to a touch of red food coloring), pink candles, a pink cake, pink coleslaw, pink lemonade, pink whipped cream for the strawberries, pink candies thrown on the tables and, of course, all the guests were invited to wear pink.

"Tweenage" Party ⊚ If your nine- to twelve-year-old is at that in-between stage—not quite a teen, yet no longer a little child—throw a tween-age party. Rent the local gym and provide a multi-dimensional party with basketballs, hula hoops, and other athletic gear at one end, and music and dancing at the other end. The kids will have a blast and nobody will feel uncomfortable at being put in too childish or too grown-up a situation.

Sweet Sixteen ⊚ A surprise party for our daughter Ali when she turned sweet sixteen was a huge hit. The centerpieces were made of candy, from chocolate high heel shoes to giant lollipops. We had a large sheet cake created that was a replica of her driver's license—with her photograph and all the pertinent information. How sweet it was!

Adult Parties

No One Can Fill Your Shoes ⊚ When I turned fifty, I threw a party for fifty of my favorite people, from family to friends. To surprise everyone, I had the lunch plates put in gift boxes and each wrapped up with a pretty bow. When the guests arrived, they were all astounded that there was a large gift at each person's place setting. My aunt even put hers under her chair to save and open later. When they learned it was their lunch, they were completely shocked! The theme of the party was "No one can fill your shoes," and here's the poem that was written on the invitation:

> *Robyn's turning fifty*
> *Half a century old.*
> *And in her book of those she adores*
> *You're one of her favorite souls.*

Because you are someone important
And etched in her heart through time.
You are one of those special individuals
Who is the reason for this rhyme.

Please accept this invitation
You're someone she would choose.
To celebrate her momentous occasion,
And no one else can fill your shoes!

You Old Fool © Have someone you want to really fool with a surprise party? Throw one in his or her honor on April Fool's Day. Invite people to really fool him by celebrating his birthday early or late. Say, "He's no fool on his fortieth, so let's fool him in his fortieth year." The surprise is sure to be most unexpected and you have a chance to mark the occasion in a fun and memorable way.

It's A Beach Party © This summertime beach-themed party is especially fun. Re-create a beach setting with beach umbrellas, beach balls, and towel tablecloths. Decorative kites can be placed around the dance floor for additional color and excitement. The entrance could be heavily embellished with fish, tropical trees, boardwalk, and inflatable inner tubes and blow-up dolphins, and other colorful pool accessories. White beach chairs add a final appeal to the room, along with nautical flags and life preservers with the honoree's name on them.

Get-Organized Party © One of my favorite ideas of all time is to throw a busy friend a get-organized party. Begin by bringing an address book and circulating it around the party so that guests can add their addresses, e-mails, cell phone numbers, birthdays, anniversaries—the works for that special honoree who either loves being organized or needs to be more organized. Party favors can include address labels you make with each person's name and address on them.

Black Tie Billiards © The Pickardo Invitational is the yearly gathering of four couples who get together at The Pickard's home to play pool, eat indulgently, and try to win the highest honors as pool sharks that evening. The team not shooting pool plays Pictionary and the games go on into the wee hours of the morning until there's a winner.

All In The Family ⓒ Joan Weiss shared a memorable party she threw for a close friend's special birthday. She and her husband invited the couple, with their children and grandchildren, for brunch. Instead of inviting a host of friends, the family affair gave everyone a memorable treat, and let the families share in their happy day together.

Party On! ⓒ Sometimes, after a special occasion or a holiday, it's hard to come down from all of the excitement. So, party on and throw another party or celebration the week after! For example, the week after the holidays or a special occasion, plan a party to share photographs or reminisce about special memories.

Super Bowl Parties ⓒ Calling all couch potatoes for this party! When inviting guests, ask them to bring one of their favorite "TV" junk foods; but you supply the cold cuts, chili, and sandwich platters. This party will be overflowing with calories and fun, but make it really memorable by packaging up junk food doggy bags from the leftovers as a party favor. Add some extra items to your bags just in case everything is gobbled up.

Come As Your Mate ⓒ This party is ideal for a different spin on Halloween and is more enjoyable than you'll ever imagine. The secret to this party is that you'll need a fun group to pull it off! Send an invitation to come as your mate! Have a camera and designated photographer on hand and ready to take lots of pictures as each couple arrives as their significant other.

Derby Day ⓒ Call your friends to the post and invite them to gallop over for a Kentucky Derby Party. In fine Derby tradition, everyone should wear a clever hat, and guests can vote on their favorite horse. Create tickets to the track as invitations and greet everyone with racing programs listing each race along with a corresponding dinner course. End the evening on a lucky note. Serve a horseshoe-shaped cake dessert.

Suddenly Single! ⓒ One recently divorced woman threw a really memorable party to thank her friends and clients for their support during her ordeal. As her divorce was finalized, she had an open house to thank everyone for their support. She sent out an invitation that said: *It's A Suddenly Single Party! I wish to thank my friends and family for helping me through this time! Please bring a dish! No regrets allowed!*

Fashion Survivor Party ⓒ This is a really fun party with the theme of "come as you were," and "what were you thinking," and "how could you wear that?" Ask your guests these important questions and then invite them to come to a party "dressed like you were!" Have appropriate food and music from that decade (fifties, sixties, seventies, eighties, and so on), or re-create the era when you were sweet sixteen and really young at heart. Most everyone saves a blast from the past in their closet, so encourage them to come dressed as the part. Make it a festive party, take loads of photographs, and give out "Best Dressed Then" Awards.

He Did It His Way! ⓒ Lori Simon shared the details of her dad's sixtieth surprise birthday party. "We gave the party in a restaurant, and for my dad's centerpiece, since my dad loved Frank Sinatra, I had a stand-up likeness of Frank Sinatra in a pose he is famous for. He stood with a suit, his famous hat, and his coat draped over his shoulder. I had my dad's face put on the picture with a sign above that said, 'Aaron did it his way' based on Frank's song, 'My Way.' He adored this centerpiece and saved it for over twenty years."

Been There, Bought That Party ⓒ Does she love to shop? This party will be the right match for your favorite shopaholic. Collect an assortment of colorful shopping bags from her favorite stores and place flowering plants or vases of flowers in them for a fun centerpiece. Are you on a shoestring budget? The shopping bags with colorful tissue will make a festive statement. Then surround the bags with a few purses and play money from your MONOPOLY game. The purses can also be filled with silk flowers for a fun touch. On each invitation, which has a shopping theme, of course, guests should be invited to bring a shopping tip, coupons for the super shopper, and wear their latest bargain!

Bar and Bat Mitzvahs

A Bar Mitzvah (for a boy) or Bat Mitzvah (for a girl) is a very special religious ceremony symbolizing adulthood in the life of a Jewish thirteen-year-old and it requires a great deal of studying and hard work. Most Bar and Bat Mitzvahs send an invitation to their special day and many have a theme that ties into a festive celebration that follows after sunset that evening. The key to making that party memorable is to reflect the Bar or Bat Mitzvah's accomplishments and interests and personalize it.

Book Mitzvahs © The theme of one Bat Mitzvah was a book mitzvah, which continued the tradition of performing a mitzvah or good deed. In honor of her guests the Bat Mitzvah girl donated a children's book to her day school with bookplates commemorating her special event. Each guest's place card indicated the book that was donated in their honor and the centerpieces were buckets of the books on pedestals with balloon bursts coming out of them.

Saturday Night Live! © One of the most memorable Bar Mitzvah parties ever was "Saturday Night Live with Blake Simon." Blake was a thirteen-year-old who hosted his Bar Mitzvah video and party as the MC. A talented pianist, he also starred as the musical guest for the evening with a Saturday Night Live theme. Blake's parents wanted his celebration, which included dinner and dancing, to display his special qualities and talents. From the moment you arrived, you were swept up in the excitement of live television, all centered around Blake. Blinking lights and Blake's "publicity shot" were featured on the signs announcing the taping at 8:00 P.M. on August 30, 2003. Guests were ushered into a video screening room that simulated an actual taping of Blake's Saturday Night Live with flashing applause lights and On-Air signs. An MC prepared everyone for the taping, and then the video began that reenacted Saturday Night Live vignettes, only starring the Bar Mitzvah boy. The audience howled, but they were touched by the sentiment, and the video was a huge success, ending with thunderous applause.

Blue Jean Bar Mitzvah © A causal party was the ideal celebration for one Bar Mitzvah boy who liked to only wear jeans. The evening's celebration was a jeans-only party, but your best jeans! No dresses, tuxes, or suits allowed. Denim tablecloths set the tone for this festive affair, place cards were in denim pockets that held the table assignments, and the casual atmosphere was both comfortable and enjoyed by all who attended.

Bark Mitzvah © If your Bar or Bat Mitzvah boy or girl really loves animals, and has a dog, make the boy or girl and their dog the theme of the evening. Do what one family did and call it a "bark mitzvah" and play out the party theme around his or her precious pooch.

I Dream Of Gena! ◎ Marcy Solmson shared with me one of the cutest themes I'd heard about in a long while, it was created by her company Event Savvy for a recent Bat Mitzvah party for a girl named Gena. The theme of her festive party was *I Dream Of Gena*. Decorations ranged from genie lamps to hot pink tablecloths. Centerpieces were surrounded with items she dreamt about, including her favorite sports, interests, and hobbies. This clever idea could also work for Joanie, Gina, Jenny, or any other name that sounds similar to Genie.

Candy Bar Mitzvah ◎ If you want to have a Bar or Bat Mitzvah with a candy theme, and your child loves junk food and candy, this is a fun party that pleases guests of all ages. Cover a long bar at the party with loads of candy of all shapes and sizes. Have stacks of small cups that the guests can fill up and enjoy. Add a sign that says, "Ali's Sweet Cart" or "Justin's Candy Bar Mitzvah."

The Secret Garden ◎ A meaningful Bat Mitzvah party was centered on a fantasy theme and the book *The Secret Garden*. This Bat Mitzvah party was transformed into a garden-like setting, but what made it so special was that all the plants that were used as the centerpieces and decorations were donated and later planted by the girl's family at a local senior citizen's home that needed sprucing up.

A Real Mitzvah ◎ The word Mitzvah is Hebrew and it means "a kind deed." One Bat Mitzvah illustrated this in the most generous way. In lieu of an evening party, the girl's family donated a playground to her synagogue. Another Bar Mitzvah funded a scholarship to help a less fortunate child attend overnight camp. Think about ways that your Bar or Bat Mitzvah party celebration can make a difference. Consider using plants as centerpieces and donating them in honor of your Bar or Bat Mitzvah, or even your guests.

is for Quick and Easy Gifts You Can Make Yourself

Over twenty years ago, I had the pleasure of teaching art to elementary school students, and the biggest challenge was that our school had limited resources and a tight budget for art materials. However, that circumstance, which could have potentially limited success, became my greatest accomplishment. I discovered so many exciting and novel ways to create crafts by recycling things in our environment and turning trash into really beautiful treasures. It never ceased to amaze me how my students would create works of art from things you might otherwise have thrown away. These pint-sized Picassos illustrated that everything that's old can be new again!

While years have passed from those days of teaching art, I continue to love adding my personal touch to everything I do. As a mom, I have taught my children how to create gifts that are inexpensive and that they can make themselves. As a "quick crafter," I keep a stable of supplies on hand—like permanent markers, self-sticking alphabet letters for instant personalizing, and other basics like glue sticks, loads of stickers, and odds and ends. This chapter is one of my favorites because it serves as a reminder that, when you make something yourself, a piece of you is a part of that gift forever.

Gifts For Kids To Make

Ticket Tape Bowls © The first time I saw our daughter, Ali, create this bowl I was absolutely surprised. Within seconds, she transformed a large roll of "admit-one" tickets into a fabulous bowl. Here's how: First, she purchased a roll of admit-one tickets that are sold at business supply stores. (They are available in red, white, and blue and very inexpensive.) To instantly make the bowl, she pushed evenly in the center of the roll of the tickets while pulling up the sides to form the desired shape. The more she pulled on the sides of the roll, the taller the bowl got. For a personalized touch, she collaged the bowl's sides with magazine clippings and fun words that fit a special friend's personality. She left the admit-one tickets showing on the top rim. The glue used to connect the collaged pieces makes the bowl very sturdy and holds the ticket roll in place. Ali created one of the cutest gifts I've ever seen.

Egg Carton Creations © Egg cartons provide a quick and inexpensive container that can be recycled into a clever craft. Since it's the perfect catch-all container, transform it into a jewelry box by decorating the top with someone's name using self-sticking letters and other odds and ends. If kids also create a piece of jewelry, give it in an egg carton container for a "gift in a gift" and a special surprise. Or, cut a strip from an egg carton and add eyes from odds and ends, soda caps, pipe cleaner legs and—before you know it—egg carton creatures!

Uncanny Containers © Clean cans without sharp edges are great to craft with. When kids are doing the crafting, an adult should clean the can, tape the edge with electrical or duct tape, and then let the fun begin. Cover the can with pretty gift-wrap papers or collage it using a variety of papers left over from opening other gifts. Using the scraps from a special event to cover a can to hold pencils, etc., makes a special reminder of a happy time. With self-sticking letters, add the recipient's name, or your name.

It's Totally Clear © I learned this trick from our daughter Ali. She showed me an easy way to make a collage—she created one from magazine clippings, and it looked shellacked, but without the smell and fuss. Ali takes clear packaging tape, which is sold at office supply stores, and cuts pieces to cover her work. She layers the tape covering her image. It gives the surface a shiny finish and protects her work. Collaged boxes, bottles, containers, bulletin board frames, and more, make great gifts.

Paper Clip Jewelry ◎ Hook a series of paper clips together to make a necklace that's long enough. Once the necklace's length is formed, take pretty self-sticking papers, and let kids wrap the paper around the clips to transform it into a stylish accessory. These also work well when making decorative rings to serve as napkin rings.

Bottle Cap Refrigerator Magnets ◎ Recycle bottle caps by cleaning and drying them, and then fill them with photographs that will put a smile on anyone's face. Search through old photographs that aren't in scrapbooks and look for images that are too small to appreciate. These are the perfect scale. Then all you have to do is trace the cap around the photo, cut it out, and place a piece of tape or light coat of glue in the cap, and press the photo in for a snug fit. Add a piece of magnetic tape to the back of the cap for fun fridge décor.

Greeting Card Creations ◎ Since I'm a huge greeting card fan, it's natural that I save every card that is sent to our family. I have boxes and bags filled to the brim, and they've become a great place to discover fabulous crafting materials for clever hangtags, and for decorating gift-wrapped packages, fun bookmarks, and even book reports and posters that need sprucing up. A favorite craft we do with these cards is to take a notepad that has a paper cover, or a plain address book, and collage the cover with someone's name. We then cut out pieces from the cards they've sent over the years, their handwriting, words of expressed love, and glue them on. Using clear packaging tape, the surface is sealed for the finishing touch.

Gifts For Adults

(Older kids can do many of these projects, but adults should always supervise, and make sure the projects are age-appropriate when working with younger children.)

Trash Bag Flowers ◎ One of my favorite ideas of all time is to create carnation flowers from white trash bags. Cut open the trash bag so you have one large piece of plastic. Then, cut the trash bag into three-inch-wide strips (or the size you prefer) that is the length of the bag. Any length bag works from small to large. Next, thread up a needle with a long thread and tie the end in a knot. Begin stitching along the bottom side of the trash bag edge with an over and under stitch. As you sew you'll begin gathering the edge and twirling the plastic so that it forms a spiral and begins to create your flowers. Then, once you reach the end and you've formed a flower, knot the thread so that it doesn't come loose. These "fun" flowers are fabulous for topping gifts, making bouquets, corsages, and more, on a shoestring budget.

It's In The Bag ◎ Take a box of tissues, and wrap it like a gift, only leave one end open. Carefully slide your fingers down each edge to crease the paper so that your bag is beginning to take shape. Then trim the open end and slip the tissue box out of the form. You'll end up with a fabulous gift bag. For a super finishing touch, fanfold the top of the bag and staple it right in the center so that the fan opens up like butterfly wings on top of the bag.

Paper Clip Holders ◎ Clean an empty can carefully, dry it, and then tape the edge with electrical or duct tape to keep it from being sharp. Cover the outside of the can with a pretty paper and then place a self-adhesive magnetic strip around the inside of the opening of the can. This makes a fabulous paper clip holder, just like the store-bought ones. You can also do this with a clear plastic container and decorate it with jewels or stickers.

Personalized Stationery ◎ Probably the easiest and most versatile of all gifts that you can make yourself is personalized stationery. Whether you create it on the computer with fancy fonts and then duplicate it, or collage or assemble it in some fashion, the sky is the limit. My favorite stationery was just a little black-and-white sketch our daughter Ali had made when she was a little girl. It was a stick figure holding flowers. I photocopied it and printed off sets at a quick-copy store. Other fun ideas include: a creative use of the person's initials, putting inspiring quotes on cards, words like "Too Fabulous," or favorite expressions. You can also add card enhancers like little silk flowers, buttons, and odds and ends that can be found at craft and card stores.

Pad It! © Another super-clever idea that is underestimated and a fantastic gift is to have notepads created. A service available at quick-copy stores, you'll try this once and then many more times in the future. Begin by checking out your options for padding, and then design a page so that it makes an initial impression either with the person's name, hobbies, interests, or initials. You can have every page repeated or create a decorative cover for your pad that's really memorable. Most will pad them so that the paper tears off one sheet at a time, and you can personalize pads for every occasion. From small pads, big pads, purse pads, notepads, to party favors, and more, this is a fabulous gift you can easily make that's also inexpensive.

Glamour Hammers © Here's an idea that's an instant success. Prime the wooden handle of a hammer and let it dry. Then, using a variety of colors and patterns, paint the handle so that it's transformed into a work of art. Perfect patterns include stripes, polka dots, or red, white, and blue for a patriotic hammer. Reflect your gift recipient's favorite colors or style and you'll be amazed at how an ordinary five-dollar hammer turns into a memorable gift that will be enjoyed forever. Include a container of picture hangers for an added touch. You can also do this with broom handles, or plungers, and create an entire designer set of do-it-yourself accessories.

Compute Up A Cookbook © Here's a quick and easy way to create a cookbook. Surf the web for a specific food type that someone special really enjoys—ranging from low-carbs to high protein to a particular style of cuisine—and create a cookbook for personal use from recipes you find that are available to be printed out and duplicated. This instant cookbook will be a favorite for a friend and customized to suit their taste. Bind it and create a personalized cover to jazz it up. You can also add photographs you've snapped and mixed in the book with special quotes and messages for an added touch.

Birdhouse Magic © Unfinished plain birdhouses offer a wonderful gift your entire family can transform. They make fabulous gifts, and colorful centerpieces or accessories, and if you want the gift to be just for the birds, then check into what types of paints will be bird-friendly and suitable for your outdoor climate. Combine a painted birdhouse with birdseed for a great gift.

R

is for Really Romantic Ideas

omance is the language of lovers. Whether you just started dating, or you are head-over-heels and madly in love with someone remarkable, keeping that excitement and creative passion going is key. With a little creative footwork mixed with extreme thoughtfulness, being romantic is easy. When you express your feelings to a significant other, the goal is to make them really feel special. Those little "I Love You"s matter a great deal, and it's important to share them throughout the year, and not limit them only to special occasions or just to Valentine's Day.

This chapter presents a variety of ideas that have worked for other couples in love. Remember, it's not always the most expensive gifts that go down in romantic history, but the little gestures you do over and over on a daily or weekly basis that win his or her heart. While you might have to work at being romantic around the clock, here's hoping that you'll be inspired by a few of these ideas. Move over Cupid! Here you come!

Just Dating

Of All The Fish In The Sea © Lindsay Roberts shared a clever idea with us, one that her roommate, Becky, had for her brother when he wanted to ask his date to Homecoming. She suggested that he buy a big fish bowl, and fill it with a bunch of live goldfish, and write a card that says, "Of all the fish in the sea, I chose you to go with me, to Homecoming 2003. Love Michael."

Forever In My Heart ⓒ Katy Schreiner shared, "When I was a senior in high school, I was unable to attend my Homecoming Dance because my grandmother passed away. I was very upset—not only at the fact that my grandmother had died, but also that I was going to have to cancel all my plans for the dance. My boyfriend completely understood, and took me out to dinner the night before I left for the funeral, and bought me flowers. However, that was not all. A couple of days before Valentine's Day, my boyfriend called and asked me to check my car to see if he had left his wallet there. When I walked out the door I saw a rose with a note attached from my boyfriend, and he asked if I would join him for dinner at a fancy restaurant on Valentine's Day to make up for me missing the dance. I was able to wear the dress I bought for Homecoming and get all dressed up with someone I really cared about. Three and one-half years later, we are still together, and I will never forget that simple gesture."

A Treasured Hunt ⓒ Eighteen-year-old friend Carly Heyman shared this memorable moment. She said, "It all began when my best friend wanted to do something extra-special for her boyfriend for their one-year anniversary. (Keep in mind; dating for a year in high school is a very important celebration!) She didn't want to give the ordinary gifts: teddy bears, candies, and balloons. So, we got creative, and created an enormous, thoughtful, and personalized scavenger hunt. We carefully selected our destinations—places that symbolized their relationship; for example, the first place they kissed, his soccer field, the rock they always climbed, their favorite restaurant, etc. Then, at each location, we hid a card containing the unforgettable moment they shared together at that place, along with a cute riddle that gave him clues to his next destination."

Movie Magic ⓒ Take her to a totally sappy, romantic movie and slip her a small wrapped gift to open in the middle of the movie. Select something really special like a diamond heart, heart of gold, or a pendant necklace. She'll never forget your cinema surprise!

A Homecoming Memory ⓒ Lindsay Roberts shared a special memory that her entire high school probably remembers. She recounts, "My friend Mark was on the varsity football team, and he asked his girlfriend to go with him to Homecoming in front of our whole school at a pep rally. The football team sits on the gym floor during pep rallies and Mark got up toward the end of the rally to introduce the team to the school. When he was finished, he called his girlfriend down from the stands to the floor. When she was standing next to Mark, the whole team ran over and, in unison, bent down on their knees and whipped out aviator sunglasses, and sang, "You've Lost That Loving Feeling." When they finished, Mark asked her to the dance. The school loved it."

Spell It Out © From cereal, to alphabet pasta, to candy hearts or letters, spell out your love for your sweetie. You can glue the letters to a cardboard box, or—one of my favorite ideas—just put them in a special container and challenge her to unscramble it to figure out the message. From "Will you go to the prom?" to "I love you more today than yesterday" it will be fun and a very meaningful gesture.

Can't Bear To Be Without Her? © Tell her so with a stuffed bear, only make sure that bear is holding a special love letter from you. You could also pierce the bear's ears with earrings, add a heart-shaped necklace to go around its neck, or have him holding a box of chocolates.

Romantic Gestures And Gifts

Stars In Her Eyes © If your mate loves watching the stars in the sky, consider purchasing a high-tech telescope and, at the same time every night, gaze at the stars together. Tell her, "I only have eyes for you," and when you give her the telescope tell her you have stars in your eyes and they are all thanks to her.

A Romance Renewal © If he pays a little too much attention to the bills and work, don't despair! Send him a fake bill that looks like the real thing, only it's a "Romance Renewal Notice." Don't suggest you may be "past due," but be creative, and get him to renew your romance forever. Copy one of your bills and use its language, so he can renew his romance with you, no money down.

Limo To Go © For the ultimate date hire a limousine equipped with a VCR or DVD player for a few hours. Fill it with his or her favorite foods, rent a great love story or a favorite comedy, and enjoy your movie on the move. End the date with a candlelit romantic dinner at a restaurant or at home.

Move Over Fred Astaire ◎ Dancing lessons really work. When someone teaches you how to sway to the music and avoid those two left feet, it's a romantic interlude to say the least. Surprise him or her with lessons and stick to the plan. Before you know it, they'll be calling you Ginger Rogers and Fred Astaire.

A Rhyme Every Time ◎ One of the most romantic things you can do is to write each other poetry and rhymes. One couple I met exchanges poems every anniversary and they have become priceless treasures for over fifty years. Here's one the husband wrote to his wife that they shared with me:

You're everything I could wish for in a wife,
You brighten my world, you light up my life.
And through the years I can say,
I love you more each and every day.

Perfectly Positive ◎ Give her a coupon with a promise to change one bad or annoying habit. From cracking your knuckles to interrupting, pour on the promises, and stick to it. This might not sound romantic, but it's a guaranteed way to spell out how committed you are to her happiness.

Computer Screen Supreme ◎ Design an "I Love You" screen for her computer and add a photograph of the two of you with a quote or words of affection. Or, add a compliment like "Hello Beautiful." This will definitely score points.

Take A Massage Class ◎ If your mate loves a great foot or back massage, take a class and perfect your talents. It's an easy thing to do and will be appreciated more than you'll ever know. Now he can have his own masseuse on call, and it's also a totally romantic gesture.

How Are You . . . Really? ◎ One of the kindest questions you can ask your partner is how he or she is doing—if you're *really* sincere about it. So, when you ask how he or she is, add the word *really*, and then *really* listen, *really* mean it, and *really* care.

A, B, Cs of Love ⓒ

A is for always, hear me shout.
B is for beauty—inside and out.
C is for how I care for you,
D is your dedication to all that you do.
E is for everything you are to me,
F is for the best friend there could ever be.

(You get the gist . . . now your job is to finish it! Make it memorable!)

A Garden Of Love ⓒ My dear friend H. Jackson Brown, Jr., author of *Life's Little Instruction Book,* told me about a particularly wonderful and sentimental gift that he gave his wife Rosemary. He placed flower and vegetable seeds in an envelope, and wrote messages of love on each one. For example, on a package of beets, he wrote, "My heart always beets for you." After giving Rosemary a large selection of tokens of his love on these little packages, he had them framed. His garden of love now hangs in their kitchen and is a constant reminder of his affection.

On Vacation ⓒ To surprise her with an incredible trip to a spa or special destination, begin by making a sign that says "On Vacation." Hang the sign on the door of her office (or kitchen) and surprise her by arranging every last detail ahead of time—from securing her boss's approval to lining up responsible babysitters. Then, whisk her off to someplace fabulous. Pack her bag, be sure to line up the backups, and make your list and check it twice so she will have nothing to worry about while the two of you are away!

A Special Signature ⓒ Whenever you sign a card or letter written to your mate, sign it with a meaningful closing that's just between the two of you. YSF stands for *Your Sweetheart Forever.* Or, IWLYF which stands for *I Will Love You Forever.*

Happily Ever After ⓒ Give her a copy of *Cinderella* along with a glass slipper filled with chocolate kisses. Then promise to be her Prince Charming and that she'll live happily ever after.

Come Away With Me ◎ Give a copy of the CD by Norah Jones called *Come Away With Me* and attach a brochure to a fabulous place your soul mate has always wanted to go. Include two tickets or, if you can't afford it, give her an IOU and a promise to go when you can.

Creative Proposals

Plane Passion ◎ Planning a trip with your potential bride-to-be? Talk to the airline ahead of time and have the captain of your flight recite your marriage proposal to your sweetheart over the intercom. You can just picture it: "We are now flying over the Grand Canyon and will be arriving at our destination in approximately forty-five minutes. And, by the way, Joanna, Michael would like to know if you would do him the honor of marrying him." You can even practice your walk down the aisle as you deplane with your betrothed.

Highway To Heaven ◎ Just imagine driving down the road and seeing a billboard that says "Carolyn, will you marry me?" If the billboard is near an exit with a park or other picnic stop, you can add "Exit here for yes." This purchase takes some serious planning and must be arranged ahead of time with a company that rents billboards. Pack a romantic picnic with sparkling cider for a first toast to your engagement.

Hollywood Screen Kiss ◎ For the movie buff, theater advertising has become a regular part of the experience. Buy space at the theater where you plan to propose. Right before the previews, one frame simply displays the words: "Maria, will you be my wife?" Although this is not likely to win you an Oscar nomination, it will certainly win her heart.

Shout It Out Loud ◎ Tell the world you still love your love. Take out an ad in the Sunday paper. Have your message flashed on the big screen at the ballpark. Print a bumper sticker. Fill the front yard with heart-shaped Mylar balloons. Sponsor a day on public radio in your love's name. Then turn on the radio, take him to the ball game, drive her by the billboard, and reinforce the message:

"I love you so much—this fact is so—
Now I want the whole world to know."

Stamp Of Approval ◎ Here's what one shy gentleman did for his future wife that was very memorable. He placed a love stamp on top of the box that held the engagement ring and added a note that said, "Everything about you has my stamp of approval. Will you marry me?"

A Walk In The Park ◎ Propose to her with a memory that will last forever! Purchase a white wooden park bench and have your proposal painted on it, like our friend Arthur did for his wife, Lori. Place the park bench in a visible location, like a park or yard, and take your sweetheart for a walk. When she comes upon the bench she'll be swept off her feet in no time. Arthur's proposal meant so much to Lori, every time they've moved the bench has gone with them.

Staged To Remember ◎ When my brother-in-law, Sam, proposed to Gena Gold, he prearranged it onstage at The Alliance Theater in Atlanta. They had tickets for a show and after the play, an announcer indicated it was time for a raffle. The lucky winner was Dr. Sam Spizman. Sam made Gena go up onstage with him to accept the prize and before she knew it, she was sitting in a chair and he was down on one knee proposing to her. Gena said yes and the entire audience cheered and applauded!

Nothing great in the world
has been accomplished without passion.
—Hegel

S
is for Special Days and Holidays

Everyone looks forward to those special days—holidays and commemorative occasions. Each holiday or special occasion offers us opportunities to create meaningful family traditions, which are gifts in themselves. We preserve our favorites in our minds and hearts and often count the days until they arrive.

I'll never forget creating a Valentine's mailbox for exchanging valentine cards when I was a little girl, or going trick-or-treating on Halloween with a pillowcase, since one year my bag broke! I recall the beautiful silver centerpiece filled with nuts, raisins, and candy at Aunt Freeda's house every Thanksgiving and playing hopscotch during the holidays when we gathered at my Grandma and Grandpa Freedman's house. Just name the occasion and a memory pops up! I fondly recall endless celebrations, traditions, and holidays, and they remind me of special times shared with those I care about most. These memories are linked with holidays and the repetition of them throughout the years has given me enormous comfort and pleasure.

Since there are thousands of holidays, it'd be impossible to mention every one of them, so visit the Chase's Calendar of Events at www.chases.com, which has a day-by-day list for you to check out. Invent your own traditions, pass on those you treasure most, and explore the ideas highlighted in this chapter to help make those special days memorable. (Refer to "C is for Christmas and Chanukah" and other related sections for additional gift ideas for special days.)

Special Customs Around The World

There are many customs around the world that make gift-giving more memorable, but each country dictates a different philosophy. You want to be memorable, but in a really positive way. So, here are a few to take into consideration. Eight is considered one of the luckiest numbers in Chinese culture and if you receive or give that number of any item, it's considered a gesture of good will. Avoid giving gifts of knives or scissors for, to the Chinese, this suggests the severing of a friendship or other close bond. In France, if you give flowers, remember that red roses are for lovers. Also, a bouquet should be given in odd numbers of flowers, in accordance with an old European tradition.

January ⊚

New Year's Day. Have a "come once you get up" party! What a fun idea for celebrating the first day of January, which begins the Western calendar year, and is a special day to get together. It's also a day for New Year's resolutions. One clever family collected everyone's resolution as they arrived to their annual party, put them and their names on slips of paper, and placed them in a coffee jar. The following year, when they sent their invitations, they included last year's resolution in the envelope.

Martin Luther King's Birthday. Observed on the third Monday in January, Martin Luther King Day celebrates the birthday of the great civil rights leader. Recite and discuss Martin Luther King's "I Have A Dream" speech, and consider creating a family peace treaty. Talk about what that really means and how you can spread good will and kindness to others.

February ⊚

Groundhog Day. On February second, the groundhog emerges from his den, and the tradition holds true. It happens every year. Punxatawney Phil peeks out from his "hole" and looks for his shadow. Celebrate the little guy's big day and serve groundhog food—lettuce and carrots—with a creative twist: carrot cake, lettuce wraps, etc. You can show the movie *Groundhog Day*, or you can take bets and make your own predictions.

Valentine's Day. Look out, Cupid, here comes your day! Valentine's Day is a day for lovers, but the key is to make someone feel super-special and totally adored. Start a special memory with a loving cup or trophy. Present it to your mate on Valentine's Day and start a tradition. The rule is to pass the loving cup back and forth each time one of you does something super-sweet. For a fun twist on celebrating Valentine's Day with children, plan a Valentine's Social. Let the kids make chocolate-dipped strawberries—some to eat on the spot, plus a special one for each child to take home. Bake or buy cupcakes frosted with plain icing, and allow the kids to decorate them with various toppings.

Presidents' Day. The third Monday in February celebrates the combined birthdays of Presidents Washington and Lincoln. On this special day, choose a president of some company you value or appreciate, and write him or her letter. Celebrate the birthdays of great leaders from the past by acknowledging leaders in the present. Or, in the tradition of our presidential forefathers, pay tribute to the founding forefathers of your family, and create a family tree documenting who's who.

March ©

The Luck Of The Green. St. Patrick's Day, the day of the Irish, is celebrated on March seventeenth. There are many customs that make this day one to share—from wearing green so you'll be kissed to wearing orange and getting pinched. Start a tradition: each year prepare a memorable meal that's all green! You'll be surprised how much fun this is, from spinach pasta to salad, vegetables to lime-green pudding, and mint green ice cream.

Spring Is Sprung. The vernal equinox, the first day of spring, occurs on March 20, 21, or 22, depending on the year. Throw a Spring Fling Feast and serve seasonal vegetables, fruits, and a colorful dinner with flowers galore and everything in season.

April ©

April Fool's Day. Create an invitation that says something wild like "Congratulations, you have won the lottery." On the inside of the invitation, write . . . "If you are foolish enough to believe this, you are the perfect guest at our April Fool's Day Dinner on _____." Or, how about a foolishly formal party? Invite your friends for an evening of fools on April 1st. Everyone must come dressed formal or foolish . . . or foolishly formal. Send out silly invitations written upside down or backwards. You can even write invitations with invisible ink and send a decoder marker to make the writing appear.

Secretary's Day. Give your secretary something that tells her that her bright ideas are really valued. Ask everyone in the office to participate in "Surprise Our Secretary" Day and bring in little surprises to secretly leave on her desk during the day. The key is, you can't be caught giving her the gift. Also, brighten her desk with pretty flowers in a colorful vase, and add a note that says, "Your hard work and bright ideas make our day!"

Easter. The most famous basket of all time is the traditional Easter basket that is filled with chocolate bunnies, Easter eggs, and other sweets and gifts that celebrate this beloved holiday. For a memorable idea, start a *Some Bunny Loves You* collection, and include a glass or china rabbit keepsake in the baskets you give everyone. Write the year on the bottom of the bunny with a permanent marker.

Passover. Passover, or Pesach, is a Jewish holiday that tells of the liberation of the Jewish people from slavery in Egypt. It lasts eight days, during which time no bread or leaven is eaten. A really fun tradition Linda Reisman and her family has for Passover, is to have the adults dress up as Moses and Pharoah (beards, sheets, sandals), and have them act out the "Let my people go" part of the story for the young children. They played taped music of the "No, No, No, I will not let them go" song and made paper-plate depictions of the ten plagues. To include everyone, they give them out to the kids so each child is responsible for pretending to be a plague or two.

May ©

Cinco De Mayo. This Mexican national holiday celebrated on May 5th is filled with festivities, parades, and special traditional foods. Fill a basket with musical instruments, noisemakers the kids can make from paper towel tubing, and add hot sauces and Mexican specialties for a memorable gift.

Mother's Day. Mother's Day falls on the second Sunday in May. Research companies who create photo keepsakes. Have Mom's children put charms on the keepsakes and tell her she's the most "charm-ing" mom around. Or, call her every hour on the hour if you're away. You can also give Mom a list of activities and assign each family member one that she chooses. Her day will begin and end spending time with her favorite crew. Or, how about a lottery bouquet for Mom? Tell Mom you hit the jackpot with her as a mother, or say how lucky you feel to have her as your mother. Create flowers out of tissue paper, roll up lottery tickets or instant scratch off games, and stick them in the centers. She's already a winner with kids like you!

Memorial Day. Originally May thirty-first, Memorial Day is now celebrated on the last Monday in May. On this day we remember and honor those who gave their lives in service to their country. Find a family who lost someone during the war and create a family project that would pay special honor to their memory. Honor them by writing letters of gratitude to their family.

June ☺

Father's Day. The third Sunday in June is Father's Day. Dads deserve an award every day for all they do for us, so here's a special way to tell him how much he means to you. From dads to grandfathers to special uncles, or other men in your life, this idea is ideal for everyone: design and give out Family Academy Awards with the Best Dad (Grandpa, Uncle) going to . . . your dad or family member. You can create your awards on the computer and present them on Father's Day. Then fill a file folder with more awards that allow you to customize and thank Dad whenever the moment arises during the following year for outstanding performances as a dad. Here's a sample:

The Academy of Family Awards Presents To _____ The World's Best Dad In Appreciation Of The Thousands Of Hours, Monetary Contributions, And Boundless Love You Have Bestowed On Your Family.

First Day Of Summer. On June 20, 21, or 22, summer officially begins. It's also the longest day of the year, and that makes it a fun opportunity to express your feelings for someone, since there'll be no longer day in history than this one! Make a list of all the beaches across the world and a list of all that you want to visit during your lifetime with your significant other or family.

July ©

Independence Day. On the Fourth of July, one of our most festive family days, we pull out the red, white, and blue, and see fireworks, and honor our country. Start a book that tells your family's history and something about each family member. Using white icing, blueberries, and sliced strawberries, let the kids create an American flag cake for fun. Or, you can use a store-bought cake for this yearly patriotic display, and top it off with the flag's details in icing and berries.

August ©

Sister's Day. This special day occurs on the first Sunday in August, and is a day when you have an opportunity to let that special sister of yours know how much you love her. Make it a plan to get together and do something sisterly and special—from visiting a new landmark in your town, visiting the museum and sharing your love of art, or going out to dinner for comfort food just like Grandma used to make when you were little.

September ©

Labor Day. Labor Day, the first Monday in September, is a time to thank others for the fruits of their labor. Dedicated to the social and economic achievements of American workers, it's a time to celebrate with family and friends. Consider writing thank-you notes to individuals you might have forgotten, or to those people who grace your life with their support. Thank each of them for their hard work and efforts on your's and your family's behalf.

Grandparent's Day. Following Labor Day, the first Sunday in September is National Grandparent's Day. Invite grandparents over for a special skit and celebration that the children arrange and give. It's the ideal time to tell those special 'grand' people in your life how much they are loved and appreciated, and you can let the kids plan the program.

The High Holy Days. The Jewish New Year—Rosh Hashanah—and the Day of Atonement—Yom Kippur—both fall in September or October. Yom Kippur is a day of fasting (abstaining from food or drink), which ends with a special "break the fast" supper. If invited to share one of these holidays, bring a gift of food (approved by the host— and make sure you check to see if they keep kosher), or flowers. Consider sending a potted orchid or something that will be lasting to brighten their home. Gwen Bloom, of Denver, shared a family tradition that means a lot to her and her family. "During Rosh Hashanah, I bake a honey cake whose recipe was passed down from my late Aunt Rose. She was my father's oldest sister, and really more like a grandmother to me, since I had no living grandmothers as I was growing up. It is a delicious recipe, and always served with love and memories every year. Of course, we call it, "Aunt Rose's Honey Cake" and here's the recipe."

Mix Well:
3 eggs
1 cup sugar
1 cup honey
¼ cup oil

Add:
3 cups pre-sifted flour
1 tsp. baking powder
1 tsp. baking soda
1 tsp. vanilla
1 cup brewed coffee

Directions: Pour batter into well greased loaf pan. Bake at 350 degrees for 1 hour.

Serve with Memories and Love.

Signs Of Fall. Think of a creative way to welcome a change of the seasons. On September twentieth, twenty-first, or the twenty-second, autumn officially begins. One of my favorite traditions, since I was a little girl, was to celebrate the first sign of fall. Whenever I would see an acorn on the ground, I would pick it up for good luck, and knew that autumn had arrived. This little memory-maker has stuck with me forever.

October ©

Columbus Day. October 12 is Christopher Columbus's special day. What better day to take your family on a new journey and learn something new? Discover a new type of food and eat out at a restaurant that serves it, learn about America, find out about a worthwhile cause your family can help, or just do something new and intensely interesting.

Sweetest Day. Observed the third Saturday in the month of October, Sweetest Day was started to bring candy to the less fortunate. This is a fabulous time to gather a group of kids and have a pre-Halloween party, only make it memorable, and distribute candy to children's organizations.

Halloween. October thirty-first is a favorite holiday filled with fun and games, costumes, and official trick-or-treating. Make it memorable with costumes and picture-taking. Trick-or-treat for a good cause, make your own costumes, plan ahead, and consider doing what one family did every year. They took their leftover wrapped candy and covered Styrofoam balls with it, cold-glue gunning the candy onto the form and making creative centerpieces, ornaments, and goodies to give to friends and family members.

National Boss's Day. Find out the actual date for this year's Boss's Day, an October holiday. There are so many ways to honor your boss, but a fun idea is to bring into the office a surprise breakfast or brunch and honor him with a Toast. (Toasted bagels, toasted bread, and your kind words—toasted with orange juice and his favorite coffee—let him know what a great boss he is!)

November ©

Election Day. Election Day is the first Tuesday in November. Have an Election Day party, and let everyone cast a vote ahead of time, with their RSVP, of who they think will win. When the guests arrive, watch the voting precincts reporting on TV, and cheer your candidate on with an election-day supper. For dessert, write each of the candidate's names on the cake, and dish it out!

Veterans' Day. November 11 is the day we honor our veterans, those men and women who have served in the Armed Forces to protect and defend us. Do what one Girl Scout Troop did, inspired by our daughter's book titled *The Thank You Book For Kids.* They had a thank-you party and created thank-you notes in red, white, and blue, and dropped them off to a nearby veteran's hospital to express their thanks.

Thanksgiving. The fourth Thursday in November is Thanksgiving and a time to let everyone know how thankful you are by sending out thank-you notes to family, friends, and even your business contacts. Or, start a Thanksgiving tradition: on Thanksgiving we deliver toys to a nearby children's hospital and leave them at the front desk for the nurses to distribute to children who are confined to the hospital for a long period of time. My friend Lorie shared a special tradition her family does every Thanksgiving, called "The Thanksgiving Tree." Lorie added, "We have a thanksgiving 'tree' that we use each year. It's a small wooden tree with little rings from which leaves hang. We cut the leaves from construction paper, and give each person a leaf, asking them to write the thing or things for which they are most thankful. Before we begin the meal each person reads his or her leaf and them hangs it on the tree in the center of the table. We also decorate the table with pretty colored leaves from outside."

December ©

Chanukah. The Festival of Lights falls anywhere from very late November to the end of December. In the Jewish calendar, it is celebrated on the 25th day of Kislev. Chanukah means "dedication," and commemorates the victory of the Maccabees. Visit a local synagogue gift shop or Judaica store to find a varied selection of dreidels, and start a child or family member on a collection. Spin your way into their hearts during this holiday that celebrates the miracle of how the oil burned for eight days.

Ramadan. Ramadan is the ninth month of the Muslim calendar. It is during this entire month that Muslims observe the Fast of Ramadan.

Muslims fast during the daylight hours, and in the evening eat small meals and visit with friends and family. It is a time of worship and contemplation, and a time to strengthen family and community ties.

Christmas. December twenty-fifth is the day Western Christians celebrate Jesus's birth with gifts galore, holly, mistletoe, carols, and parties. Begin a tradition by baking a recipe every year and showing up with it a few days ahead of the holiday, so friends or family can serve it at their Christmas family meal. Or, if you know someone who can't go home for the holidays or must work, have a party later for them with all those leftovers you'll end up with. Here's a favorite party that caterer Tony Conway loves to give—he invites all his friends who can't go home for the holidays and indulges them with food and festivities when everyone is available. Talk about the Christmas spirit continuing!

Kwanzaa. The African American holiday of Kwanzaa lasts from December twenty-six to January first. It is a holiday affirming the accomplishments of the African American community, stressing family strength and unity. Bring homemade gifts of food, or traditional African craft objects, or items you create yourself.

Other Religious Celebrations. There are many other special days and religious occasions—ranging from Baptisms, Bar and Bat Mitzvahs, Communions to Confirmations. One tribute that is really memorable, that a friend of ours does in honor of a special occasion for a child, is to give what he calls a "check-plus." He gives a designated amount of money, and then a little extra for the child (or parents) to donate to a special cause of their choice. He commemorates their special day by giving a gift to the child, and then also encourages a portion of his gift to be given to the less fortunate.

The ornament of a house is the friends who frequent it.
—Ralph Waldo Emerson

T

is for Terrific Trips and Travel

Ask just about anyone and they'll agree that a trip is often the most innovative way to create new memories and celebrate special occasions or events in your life. They are also wonderful for building bonds and strengthening ties. Some of my most favorite memories are trips our family has taken together. The most memorable ones are always the trips when we planned our itinerary and did our homework ahead of time.

I'll never forget the story one woman told me when she received a hand-delivered card from a man who arrived at her office and serenaded her with beautiful Italian music. After he finished his repertoire, the entire office applauded and then he handed her a card that was from her husband. The card said, "You're going to flip! We're going on a trip!!" It contained two plane tickets to Italy, a place she had dreamed about going to her entire life.

The gift of travel is one of the most memorable gifts you can give away or give to yourself. With planning, preparation, and a little creativity, you can transform the experience into a memory-making masterpiece. The ideas in this chapter illustrate creative ways to help you turn your journeys into precious keepsakes and treasured memories forever.

State Of Mind. © Every state in our country can be listed in order of its admittance to the Union. One couple began at state number one, and then went to a different state that corresponded to their anniversary every year, and saw America first! On a special anniversary or birthday, consider giving a surprise visit to the state that actually coordinates with the occasion . . . a 50th birthday—visit Hawaii the fiftieth state! First anniversary? How about Delaware? Just the two of you . . . how about Pennsylvania? A family of four? Looking 4 a great time? Visit number four, which is Georgia. Here's the list in order:

Delaware—#1
Pennsylvania—#2
New Jersey—#3
Georgia—#4
Connecticut—#5
Massachusetts—#6
Maryland—#7
South Carolina—#8
New Hampshire—#9
Virginia—#10
New York—#11
North Carolina—#12
Rhode Island—#13
Vermont—#14
Kentucky—#15
Tennessee—#16
Ohio—#17
Louisiana—#18
Indiana—#19
Mississippi—#20
Illinois—#21
Alabama—#22
Maine—#23
Missouri—#24
Arkansas—#25

Michigan—#26
Florida—#27
Texas—#28
Iowa—#29
Wisconsin—#30
California—#31
Minnesota—#32
Oregon—#33
Kansas—#34
West Virginia—#35
Nevada—#36
Nebraska—#37
Colorado—#38
North Dakota—#39
South Dakota—#40
Montana—#41
Washington—#42
Idaho—#43
Wyoming—#44
Utah—#45
Oklahoma—#46
New Mexico—#47
Arizona—#48
Alaska—#49
Hawaii—#50

A Trip We Flipped Over © Television Anchorwoman Tiffany Cochran recalls a trip her father planned that she'll forever remember. She shared, "One summer my father wanted a way to get the whole family involved in a family vacation. He wanted me, my sister, brother, and grandfather to join him on a family getaway that we'd always remember. Well, I didn't think it would happen because of everyone's busy schedules, but to my surprise we all could go. He asked us to come up with our 'perfect destinations.' We all submitted our ideas—

ranging from an Alaskan cruise, to Greece, to Africa! In the end we all agreed and went to Paris, Rome, and the isle of Crete in Greece. It was an incredible gift because we were able to spend real quality time together—we climbed atop the acropolis in Greece together—and that really solidified what family means to me. Now I have the best memories of that trip and many pictures to always remind me of how much fun we had. Sometimes the best gift doesn't necessarily come in a box with a ribbon on it!"

Road Trip! © Here's a favorite trip idea that Beverly Sears shared with me. "My daughter Tasha did a really clever thing when she gave her friend Sarah a trip to remember. Tasha had purchased two concert tickets and wanted to surprise Sarah. Instead of just giving Sarah the tickets in an envelope, she created a special road trip itinerary, and mapped out their entire trip, included the tickets, concert highlights, and all the details from start to finish. Tasha made a scrapbook called 'Tasha and Sarah's Road Trip' in the tradition of the movie *Thelma and Louise,* laminated the pages, researched and included all the trip's details, ranging from pictures of the hotel they were staying at, places they'd see and visit, landmarks, sites, and more. It turned their car trip into a fabulous memory, and the road trip scrapbook was a keepsake forever."

Seattle's Flower Market © If you've never been to Seattle and walked through the famous flower market, it's an experience worth having. I'll never forget the Teddy Bear Sunflowers, and hundreds of other varieties of flowers that I'd never seen, much less heard of. Taking photographs at the market was a highlight, and the only way it could have been more memorable was if we could have taken all the flowers home on the airplane!

A Charmed Life © Charm bracelets are a great way to show where you've been and, of course, what you've bought! They also make for wonderful gifts for those who didn't get to go. Name it a "travel bracelet" and do what one mother did for herself, her daughter, and her daughter-in-law—she made bracelets all with different charms, but the same theme. This is also a wonderful thing to do for a best friend, maid of honor, or someone else really special. Begin by purchasing a silver or gold link bracelet, and over time add charms to commemorate different trips and unique features about the places you visit. These little mementos become a very meaningful keepsake for you, your family, and everyone you meet as you charm them with tales of your worldly travels.

Let It Snow! ◎ Use your travels to build a collection, like we did for our daughter, Ali. Since Ali loves the cold and snow, and we don't get too much of it in the south, everywhere we traveled we brought her back a snow dome, which were inexpensive and easy to carry. She ended up with one from almost every state in the country, and has a fun collection that she enjoys to this day. The fun thing about this memorable collection was that other family members starting doing the same thing for Ali. For example, when her Uncle Sam traveled, he brought back Ali snow domes from all over the world. Her collection sure has grown, and is a meaningful reminder of everyone who loves her, and places she can one day look forward to visiting.

Room Service Please ◎ When someone you care about is traveling, or it's a special occasion and they are staying at a hotel, check with room service to explore the creative options you can do. From sending up strawberries dipped in chocolate and a bottle of wine, which is a tried-and-true gift, to going overboard with a plate of their favorite foods (piled up high), the choices are endless.

Daily Devotion ◎ Write letters and mail them to the hotels where he/she will be staying. Add notes on the envelopes with dates to deliver or open. Have a letter for each day he/she will be gone. Even contact the hotel desk to ask that the letters be delivered one at a time. If you don't have time to write letters, inquire about the hotel's fax or e-mail service and how much they'll charge to deliver your messages. Cover the costs and send one a day.

Get Away At Home ◎ Take note of special meals shared on vacations. Recreate these meals at home every once in a while for a special get-away treat. Buy a bottle of wine from the area, listen to special music from that place, and decorate your table to match the meal.

All On Board ◎ One family surprised their dad on his sixtieth birthday by booking a trip and planning all the details with their mom. She got him to the airport under false pretenses, since he thought he was being the world's best husband and going to her high school reunion. Instead, they surprised him with a trip to a golf resort he had talked about wanting to visit for years. She fooled him by sitting at the next gate, and when it was time to board, the entire family was waiting on the plane, dressed in T-shirts that said . . . Happy Birthday Dad!

A Trip With Good Taste © If you love to eat, and you have friends who share your passion, purchase local or regional cookbooks as you travel. When you return home, have a dinner party, and prepare a selection from each book, to share. As each guest leaves, give him or her one of the cookbooks to keep.

Sensational Souvenirs © Research regional specialties before you travel. On your trip, search out regional specialties to bring home. Whenever possible, include brochures, maps, and recipes, that will bring the items to life for the recipients. Match the gift to the recipient . . . a gourmet could get maple syrup from Vermont, a lobster bib from Maine, real baked beans from Boston. A handicrafts enthusiast would enjoy handmade pottery from the Carolinas, a woven throw from Kentucky, a quilt from Virginia. A glass lover would appreciate a handblown article from West Virginia. Present your gifts with the maps and brochures, and a short note from you describing how you found them and what the surroundings were like. "As we were driving through rural Kentucky, we saw a sign pointing to a small town filled with artists. We stumbled onto a college dedicated to keeping mountain crafts alive! Pottery, woven blankets, wooden items, candles, glass . . . all absolutely gorgeous, and all made by hand by the students! And in the most breathtaking setting you can imagine, nestled in the mountains, all green and misty and too serene for words. I just had to bring a little piece of it home to you!"

A Picture Postcard Thank You © Solicit ideas for your trip before you go. Ask friends who've been there, what's happening, what's wonderful. Then, as you visit, pick up a postcard and send a thank-you note from each destination, each park or restaurant, whatever they recommended. It will be a running commentary on your trip, and a reminder to your friends of how you listened to them and how great their advice was.

Goodie Bags To Go © When someone you know is going on a long trip, pack up a goodie bag filled with their favorite mints, candies, a magazine, or information about where they are going. I did this for three friends traveling to New York on the occasion of their fiftieth birthdays. Included was candy, gum, my favorite New York resources, and tips on what sales were happening that week in New York City. I also included a postcard hanging from each bag that said, "Wish I was there!"

Miles Of Smiles © Whenever traveling with our kids on long trips, I always hung a shoe bag on the back of the seat to keep them occupied. As the trip continued and they both cooperated, they would be allowed to select a surprise from the shoe bag, which held carefully planned activities that were well-suited for a car ride—from handheld games, magnetic activities where pieces didn't get lost, to art projects that didn't make a mess and were easy to do while riding. The "shoe bag to do bag," as we called it, was a time-treasured and favorite part of our car trip travels.

Travel Blunders © Not all memories of your trips and travels are good ones but, the funny thing is, they often become your funniest memories later on. From the haunted house we named The Red Barn Inn that we stayed at in the mountains to the awful hotel we were booked at during our first trip to London that didn't have elevators (and we were on the top floor), those were some of the funniest memories ever. We always pose for photographs in front of those places we'd like to forget, and make crazy faces. If you do the same, you'll be surprised how some of your most challenging moments are your funniest memories later on.

Trips To Treasure © No one will ever forget being whisked away for a surprise trip, so do your homework and line up a surprise for someone special. One family gives the kids clues, such as the type of clothing needed, but does not disclose the destination. One husband takes his wife, every year on their anniversary, to another famous beach somewhere far away. And a group of five singles formed a Travel Club (much like an investment or book club), and they all pitched in a specific amount yearly and then met monthly to plan their trip and how to make it memorable!

A Royal Invitation © When two mothers took their daughters on a mother-daughter trip to London, instead of just telling them about the trip in a normal way, they created formal invitations from the Queen that requested their presence by Her Royal Highness. They surprised them while shopping one day and had a store manager present them. The girls jumped up and down, and screamed so loud you could hear them all the way to Kensington Palace.

Sands of Time © One grandfather who traveled often wanted to bring back something really unusual from the far away places he visited. So, he brought back a container of sand and put a small amount in several tiny glass bottles. He presented each grandchild with the sand souvenir and told them all about his travels and where the sand was from. Years later, the tradition still continues and the collection of bottles now spans the world.

The truly happy man
is one who can enjoy
the scenery on a detour.
—Anonymous

U

is for Unforgettable Words, Letters, Quotes, and Notes

The power of each spoken or written word has immeasurable reach and the ability to make a difference. I'm often reminded of the letter that my grandfather wrote my father on the day he and my mother were married, wishing them well, and reminding him to take good care of her. This letter has been carefully saved in a vault for over fifty years. His handwriting was a loving reminder of his presence, and his kind voice could be heard as you read between the lines. My mother visits the vault often to reread the letter, and it has become a treasured keepsake since he passed away over twenty years ago.

Over the years, written words of love and affection have become the cornerstone of many of my fondest memories. I am so touched by words that I have even saved hundreds of cards and letters throughout the years. Consider, for a moment—what positive, kind words have you spread to make the world a little bit kinder in your corner? How often do you express the thanks and love you feel in your heart?

This chapter presents memorable words for a variety of occasions. When you're at a loss for words or just wish to make a letter or note unforgettable, here are some choice phrases and ideas to choose from.

Adjectives And Other Words To Express Memorable Feelings

Choose From The Following List When You Want To Enhance Your Words And Describe Your Feelings ◎ Amazing, awestruck, breathtaking, commendable, compelling, dazzling, distinctive, distinguished, elegant, exceptional, experienced, exquisite, fantastic, fashionable, first-class, first-rate, generous, glamorous, gratifying, handsome, impeccable, incomparable, incredible, ingenious, inspiring, invaluable, extraordinary, lovely, magnetic, meticulous, monumental, opulent, outstanding, over-the-top, prolific, radiant, rare, ravishing, refreshing, remarkable, snazzy, stunning, stupendous, sumptuous, superior, svelte, tasteful, thoughtful, thrilling, triumphant, unmatched, unparalleled, unrivaled, well-deserved.

For Memorable Congratulations, Try These:

- Congratulations! You must be thrilled to know that you accomplished what you set out to do. None of us were surprised, though, since we knew from the start you could do it!

- We were elated to learn of your outstanding accomplishment and it did our hearts good to hear about your promotion. It couldn't happen to a more well-deserving person!

- You knocked us off our feet when we heard your good news!

- We are so delighted to learn of your exciting news—a hearty congratulations to you all!

- Wow! May your recent success be the beginning of many more to come in the near future. You've reached the rewards you so justly deserve.

- Our heartiest and warmest congratulations to someone we all adore. May your successes multiply over time and bring you the many rewards you so deserve.

- It's so nice to know that you were rewarded for your outstanding achievements. We thought you deserved this award long ago and we'll be cheering you on to continued success.

- We're in awe of all the outstanding work you've done over the years.

- We believe your future is so bright we'll all be wearing sunglasses!

For Birthday Congratulations—Try A Play On Words!

Dear _____

We'd go to any lengths to say happy birthday to you—even to the depths of the deep blue ocean! Keep; your head above water and count on us anytime. We're getting ready for the big one next year . . . that'll be a tidal wave! We wish you a sea of happiness with oceans of love!

Wishing you sunny days ahead,

_____

Memorable Openers and Greetings

Warm greetings to my favorite cousin,
My dearest sister,
Dear devoted children,
My cherished daughter,
My dear amazing son,
Greetings to our favorite cousins,
Hello to my ciao bella (beautiful girl),
Dearest sweetheart,
My one and only,
Dear special friends,

Memorable Closings To Consider

Huge hugs to you and your wonderful family,
You're in our deepest thoughts daily,
Time stands still when we are apart,
Forever yours and forever us,
Looking forward to our next get-together,
Thinking of you always and hoping to see you soon,
Hope your day is as fabulous as you are,
Affectionately yours,
With huge hugs and endless kisses,
Forever you are in my thoughts,
My heartfelt thoughts are with you,
Love in your direction,
All our love and all our wishes,
With every good wish for your well-being,
With love, your biggest fans,
We remain in awe of your success,

Words To Express Your Thanks

- How can I ever thank you for such an exquisite gift. The _____ is the ideal addition to our treasured collection of _____.

- The _____ is so gorgeous that it took our breath away. In fact, when we received your exquisitely wrapped present, we knew in an instant this was going to be a memorable gift.

- When everyone asks where we got the stunning _____, we'll be certain to tell them it was from our friends, the _____, who have such incredible taste.

- We will enjoy your contribution to our sterling silver pattern forever and look forward to sharing many happy occasions together.

- Your birthday gift was such a welcomed surprise. Not only was I hoping for some _____, but yours was prettier than I ever imagined.

- My heartfelt thanks to you for being so thoughtful. It seems as though every time I need a shoulder to lean on, you appear with an act of kindness. Sometimes I think you are a mind reader.

- Talk about snazzy! The _____ you selected for our twenty-fifth anniversary shows your relentless good taste and impeccable sense of style. Everyone will want one just like it when they see us enjoying it, and we have you to thank for such a gorgeous gift!

- This past weekend I think that I must have said "thank you" at least one hundred times. However, even if I said it five hundred more, I still would not be able to sufficiently express how grateful I am.

- I was stunned when I opened your birthday gift. The _____ was just what I always wanted!

Combine Your Words With A Token Of Your Appreciation

Thanks A Bunch (Include a bunch of flowers)

Thanks A Million (Attach your thank-you to a wallet filled with play money or the real thing!)

Warmest Thanks (Combine these words with a warm scarf or wool blanket)

Just Because (these words work well when sending a gift for no reason and just because!)

Memorable Thank-You Phrases

Thank You For The Gift ☺

- Your gift touched our hearts and put a huge smile on our faces.

- Our wedding weekend would not have been complete without you there.

- A treasured memory that will stay in our hearts was _____.

- Your generous gift was a reminder of your continued thoughtfulness and presence in my life.

- My heart was warmed with delight by your perfect gift—we will enjoy using it for many occasions. With all that you do, you are so mindful of every date and never miss a chance to express your love for us. That's a rare and beautiful quality.

- A gift that comes from the heart enters the heart, and your gift of _____ was clearly one that we will wholeheartedly treasure.

Thank You For Attending Our Wedding ©

- We were thrilled that you were able to join us at our wedding and for years to come we will treasure your wishes for our happiness.

- Thank you for your magnificent _____. We were hoping someone would give us a _____ and as if by magic, your lovely gift appeared. We hope you enjoyed our wedding as much as we did. Your gift will serve as a thoughtful reminder of our wonderful friendship and how you generously shared this special time in our lives.

- Our special day was even more special because you were there with us to witness our love and devotion to each other as we exchanged our wedding vows.

- Your presence was the perfect present at our wedding. And then to receive such a gorgeous gift of _____, you simply outdid yourself.

Thank You For Inviting Me! ©

- I felt so privileged to be included at your wedding (birthday dinner, etc.), and wish to thank you for thinking of me.
- I was thrilled to be a part of your special weekend and will remember it forever.
- Thank you again so much for inviting me to be part of such an incredible event. I will never forget it as long as I live.
- You are the ultimate host. I really felt at ease and enjoyed meeting all of your wonderful family and friends.
- You give new meaning to the word "entertaining." Your creativity is legendary and now I can attest to the fact that it's not a myth.

Thank You For The Baby Gift ©

* Your wonderful welcome to our baby _____ will absolutely be the talk of our friends and family every time she (he) wears it. What fun we'll have dressing her (him) up for many special family occasions, and you'll witness firsthand what a fabulous gift you selected for _____.

* When we received your adorable outfit for _____ with his (her) name monogrammed on it, we instantly knew the cameras would be clicking every time (he) she wears it.

* We were simply awestruck when we opened your baby gift and saw the antique rattle with baby _____'s initials. It's a priceless heirloom that touched our hearts beyond words and will be one of our prized possessions throughout time.

* How can we ever thank you for such a precious gift for _____? She'll be the cutest baby in all of _____ when she wears the pink-and-white-striped dress and matching bonnet that you sent her.

Thank You For Your Service © Here's a letter that Dr. Jim Braude received from a patient. The letter meant the world to him, and he saved it and shared it with me:

Dear Dr. Braude:

It is a year ago today that I had my first fateful appointment with you. Your thoughtful, accurate, and definitive diagnosis of my condition was the first great step in the process that led, I firmly believe, to the saving of my life. Things have gone very well for me since. The work has been continuous and good, and I'm feeling like a person who has never been ill a day in his life. I just thought I'd take a moment to let you know today how grateful I remain for your conscientiousness and care. I know you feel you were only doing your job, but the manner in which you did it on my behalf is something I shall never forget, nor will my children.

A Cameo Thank You © I saved a very memorable thank you from my friend and literary agent, Meredith Bernstein, who wished to thank me for the antique cameo pin I had sent her. She had lost her cameo and was hoping for one, so the gift was just what she wanted. Her thank-you note expressed her gratitude in a really touching way. She sent the personalized stationery I had given her last year (that was a note card in the shape of a purse with her initials added) and, as you opened the note, on one side was a photograph of Meredith stylishly wearing the cameo. She cut the photograph into a cameo shape, with a scalloped edge just like the cameo I gave her and, on the opposite side, was a little poem to express her thanks, that said:

Dear Robyn—
The Perfect Present came my way
The source, of course
I might just say . . .

Would cast her net
From stem to stern
An eye like hers
Takes no wrong turn . . .

And when at last
The brooch declared
"I am the best"
She was prepared.

So buy she did
And gifted me
A treasure fine
My thanks to thee!

When Someone Says "Don't Write Me A Thank-You Note" © I told our cousin Arlene not to write us a thank-you note for the weekend she shared with me on my fiftieth birthday, but here's the memorable 'no' thank-you note that arrived in spite of my request:

Dear Robyn:

Every detail was done to perfection but, of course, I would expect no less. And speaking of the word "no" . . . you told me NOT to write a thank-you note. So, as per your request, I won't write one. I won't thank you for the delicious dinner, and how lovely your mother was to me, and how fabulous the tables and room looked at your party. And I won't tell you how much you mean to me and how much I adore you. No, I won't tell you how appreciative I was and how much fun I had. Nope, not a chance. You won't get a thank-you note from me! No way!

Love, Arlene

Words To Express Your Get-Well Wishes ©

We hope you'll be up and moving around soon.
We'll be relieved if we hear soon that you are feeling better.
I hope this letter brightens your day.
We were deeply distressed to learn of your recent illness and hope a
    recovery is soon around the corner.
It is our greatest wish that your health will soon be restored.

Expressions Of Sorrow And Condolences ©

- We wish to extend our deepest sympathy to you and your family.

- In this time of great sorrow, we wish to express our heartfelt sympathy for the loss of _____ .

- Our entire family sends you our deepest sympathy, and our thoughts are with you at this time.

- I was deeply saddened by your news.

- A bright light has gone out due to the recent passing of your beautiful mother. We hope and pray that in due time her beloved memory will bring you comfort.

- This was such tragic news to us all to learn about your loss.

- Our words pale in comparison to the depth of your pain, but please know that we are here for you in any way possible.

- We send our most heartfelt condolences and a shoulder to lean on around the clock.

- While words have little comfort, be reassured that we remain steadfast in our support for you and offer a shoulder to lean on at any time.

Sending A Condolence Letter ◎ Our daughter, Ali, who was only sixteen, wrote this letter when her Aunt Genie's beloved father passed away.

Dear Aunt Genie (and family),

I've wanted to sit down and write you but didn't have the words to express my condolences. We are all so very sorry that your dad passed away, and I've thought a great deal about you and your family. I know this is a very hard time for you all and we send our deepest love to you. While death might just end the physical aspect of a person, their mind and soul rises and continues to survive until the end of time. Your father was a magnificent man and, now, through his memory, your sisters and the rest of your family must look beyond this obstacle and progress through life with the knowledge of the love and pride he had for each and every one of you.

As each day ends and another one starts, every day is a new beginning and outlook on life. We will cherish your dad's best qualities, and he will continue to forever live in our hearts. I love you so much and extend my condolences to you and your wonderful family.

With all my love,
Ali

Condolence Responses ◎ My childhood friend Linda wrote me this beautiful note when her mother, who we all adored, passed away. Linda's words touched me deeply.

Dear Robyn,

I wish to express my heartfelt gratitude for your help during this most difficult time. The dinner was lovely, as well as the brownies, and strawberry cake. But mostly, I thank you for your emotional support and friendship. I draw strength from the love and compassion you have shared. We can't always control all things in our lives, but knowing you are there for me when I need you is an incredible comfort. Thank you again, and I love you,

Linda

Thank You For Your Sympathy ◎

• Please accept our deepest appreciation for your thoughtfulness following our mother's passing. Your cards and visit served as a bright spot during a very dark time and brought us much comfort and love.

- We will never forget your attentive support during our recent tragedy. Your words and thoughtful deeds will be forever written in our hearts.

- Your care and sympathy will be long remembered as a token of your friendship and concern for our family. We thank you from the bottom of our hearts.

- While words fail us during this difficult time, we think of the many kindnesses you shared with our family, and wish to express our gratitude for your wishes of comfort during our time of loss and sadness.

Letters From The Heart © We've always told our children that words that come from the heart, enter the heart, and are the best gifts they can give us. So with every occasion the letters arrive and fill our hearts. While we have now saved dozens of letters, here are two examples our son and daughter wrote that touched my husband's heart.

Dear Dad,

I wanted to take this chance to write you and thank you for being the most wonderful dad in the world. As I graduated college and began law school, I went through a huge transition, and you cheered me on every step of the way. I feel comfortable where I am and it is a direct result of your diligence. I truly rely on you so much and you never let me down. I am a reflection of your success and your guidance and hope that I make you as proud as you make me. You have provided me with endless generosity and love, and I hope that one day, when I have children, I can be as helpful, guiding, and supportive as you have been to your children. You have done a great job as a person who sets positive examples, and as someone that I can talk to, re-late to, hang out with, depend on, trust, and love. You have done a wonder-ful job and I cannot thank you enough for your attentiveness and love every day of my life.

Your devoted son,

Justin

Dear Daddy,

In life there are many good things . . . many wonderful things . . . but only a few priceless things. DAD, you are one of those priceless things. I cannot express enough how much you mean to me. You are the shining star in my sky and I love you so incredibly much. You are an amazing man and such an amazing daddy. You have raised two amazing (if I might say) kids . . . and we thank you so much for who we have become to this day. Once again I love you so much, and thank God every day that you are my father and that I have you in my life.

Love, your favorite daughter in the Whole, Whole, Whole, wide world, Ali:)

A Thank-You Poem © Consider writing a poem when you wish to express your heartfelt thanks to someone. Here's an example to get you started.

You have a way of giving.
It's as special as can be.
And I'm the lucky person
Because you give that love to me.

Memorable Moments To Commemorate With Words

A Letter To Remember © There are so many moments in time when a letter wishing someone well means so much to them. Here's one story that touched me personally, one my mother has saved since 1947. Nine days before my parents were to be married, my mother's father, who passed away over twenty years ago, wrote my dad a letter that my mother has saved in the vault for over fifty years. Her father's beautiful handwriting and loving words have become a treasure that remains protected to this day. Regarding their upcoming marriage, the letter presented my father with a car for my mother, and requested my father make sure he buys a license plate and accompanying insurance for it. His concern for her safety and well-being were clear. He signed the letter, "My best regard to you, and your family and, until I see you again, I am your future father-in-law." Needless to say, every time my mom sees it, her eyes fill with tears and a special memory is relived.

Son In Love ◎ Whenever Edie Lehrner sends her son-in-law, Larry, a birthday card, she addresses it to her son-in-love. What a sweet sentiment.

Saying I'm Sorry ◎ While gifts and words won't always remedy everything, words from your heart are definitely a start. When writing an apology, make it memorable by acknowledging the problem at hand, and make sure your words illustrate that you clearly know what you did to hurt him or her, and that you wish to ask for forgiveness. If you don't know what you did, be straightforward and honest, but make sure your words reflect a loving heart, genuine apology, and the desire to make mends.

Time To Say Sorry ◎ On a lighter note, when humor is the answer, be creative in working your way out of the doghouse. Want a clever way to say you're sorry you ticked her off? Wish to tell her you're sorry about a "time" you were out of line? Give her a fabulous watch, ticking around the clock with apologies, if you know what I mean. She's bound to forgive you in no time at all!

Words At Work

Words To Work By ◎ Allen Hardin, Chairman and CEO of The Hardin Company, has some memorable practices he lives and works by. He commented that over the years he has created and built his company on two memorable mottos. The first is "There's no limit to one's success if you don't care who gets the credit," and the other one is "You'll be unique in business if you simply do what you say you'll do." Another impressionable detail that Allen shared is how he signs all of his correspondence and contracts with a felt-tip green ink pen, since green represents growth and good fortune. He loves nature, and gardens, and enjoys celebrating his passion for the color green whenever signing anything of importance. It is also memorable how Allen, like his father before him, does not allow red pens, pencils, or ink in his business because, if "you're in the red" you're losing money, and Hardin vows to steer clear of any connection to that scenario.

Quotes

Search for quotes that express your feelings, and enhance your words with words from famous people throughout time. Sometimes, words from the past are the finishing touch to help you get your point across:

"A friend is a gift you give yourself."—Robert Louis Stevenson

"Good people are remembered forever."—Psalms 112:6

"A day for toil, an hour for sport, but for a friend is life too short."—Ralph Waldo Emerson

"It is more blessed to give than to receive."—Acts 20:35

"Helping someone else is the secret of happiness."—Booker T. Washington

Nothing great was ever achieved without enthusiasm.

—Ralph Waldo Emerson

V

is for Victory Parties, Team Celebrations, and Gifts

Team players take note! There are many memorable ways you can contribute to your team besides being a good sport and great teammate. From planning parties, making favors, cheering the team on to victory, raising money, increasing the spirit, thanking your sponsors, coaches, and more, there are endless jobs when it comes to team sports, and victory celebrations.

The real victory comes in knowing that everyone who played a role in your team's efforts is appropriately thanked and knows they are appreciated. It's also about honoring the hardworking team members, on and off the bench, who dedicated time and energy to help your team show up, game after game. Team parents, family members, and friends often end up doing a great deal of work and become the behind-the-scenes heroes. However, everyone from the coach, to the water boy, to the supportive spouse knows that each person can make a huge difference to help the spirit and success of the team. This chapter addresses how to make everyone from the team members, the coach, the cheering squad, and everyone in-between, feel extraordinary and special.

Here are some ideas to celebrate those victories, efforts, and overall determination. Your team might not prevail to victory, but your parties, gifts, and efforts certainly can!

Team Parties

Traveling Team ◎ If your team travels and is flying to a tournament, bring a mild-mannered party (not too crazy, and with seat belts intact) for the airplane ride. Begin by requesting that the pilot congratulate or wish them good luck on the loudspeaker. The entire plane is bound to hear cheering as the pilot sends his high-flying wishes for their success. Next, pass out a goodie-bag for each team member, with energy bars and a special message from the coach.

"Hoop" It Up ◎ Throw a basketball brunch for the team to celebrate the beginning of basketball season. Serve pancakes, and use whipped cream to make the pancakes look like basketballs. Your big hoopla will be fun and easy. No time to cook? Even frozen pancakes and waffles will do the trick, or pick them up from a fast food restaurant and just keep them warm. If your team frequents a particular restaurant, invite the management to support your team, post your scores and player's achievements at the counter, and serve your players loads of encouragement every time they come in!

Bowl Them Over ◎ If your choice of sport is bowling, here's a fun party to have. Rent out the restaurant at the bowling alley and serve everything in—what else? Bowls! Bowls of snacks, chips, buffalo chicken wings, candy, you name it! In fact, if you are allowed to bring in food, ask everyone to bring a bowl of something. For a memorable dessert, order a cake in the shape of a bowling ball, and put all the team players' name on it, along with the coach's, for fun. For a championship celebration, add each player's highest score, if that is appropriate.

A Pom-Pom Party ◎ Ceremoniously present each cheerleader her pom-poms at a special party. Have the cheerleading squad members who make the team again do a special cheer to welcome the new cheerleading candidates who made the team. Throw this pom-pom party as a yearly tradition.

Countdown To Victory ◎ 48 Days To Victory! This is the ideal party to encourage your team to victory. Count the days to the play-offs, or championship date you are aiming at, and post how many days until the big day. You can also tie this into the school's homecoming, and countdown the days to that "big" game and weekend. To add a festive touch, when you kick off the countdown, put the number of days on a huge sheet cake and sell (or give out) pieces to raise money for your team.

A Post-Game Feast ☺ Host a pot-luck dinner and invite the entire team to come and celebrate the season by bringing a main dish or some contribution to the dinner. Call it a "post-game feast" and you'll score points with your hungry players. Talk about the season's greatest moments and give out awards for every player. From Most Applauded to Most Spirited, each and every player will appreciate being acknowledged for some special trait that they exhibited during the year.

"Fore" Golfers! ☺ This party is for golfers, and all you need to do is invite your golf team to come over for an evening of *green*. Ask everyone to bring some food that's green—from salads, to spinach lasagna, to a cake iced in green frosting. Set the table with a green tablecloth and cover it with loads of golf balls and tees.

Take Me Out To The Ballgame ☺ It's baseball time, and if you want to throw a team party, have a home-run happening. Serve up a baseball-themed dinner that will hit home with your players, and transform your kitchen or eating area into a concession stand with hotdogs, hamburgers, peanuts, cracker jacks, and all the fixings. Set it up just as you would the actual stand, and don't forget the popcorn, soft pretzels, and ice-cold sodas, bottled water, and sports drinks. Nothing's too good for your players! For a fun dessert, you can also transform chocolate-covered doughnuts to look like baseballs. Using white icing, pipe on the white stitching and other details to make each doughnut look like a baseball.

Peanut Gallery Party ☺ Throw a party for the players cheering squad—You! Invite friends and family of the players to come for a sign-decorating party. Request that players bring their friends and family to show support for the team. Entrance to the party is a poster-board, banner, or some form of a sign. Provide markers and everything necessary to decorate the signs to cheer your players on to victory.

Soccer Sub Party ☺ Invite players and their families to wear the team colors to show their support for their soccer team. Pile high those sub sandwiches, and even serve one the length of the soccer field (well, how about your table?). Order, or bake, a huge soccer ball sheet cake with all the players' names written in icing—and go for the goal.

Centerfield Centerpiece © A quick and easy centerpiece for a football party is to fill up a helmet with goodies like candy bars, bags of Cracker Jacks, and make it your centerpiece. Elevate it in the center of the table, with pom-poms around it in your team colors. When the party ends, give out the candy that filled it up, and fill up your guests with a sweet surprise.

Great Moments In Sports © From a Volleyball Mania Dinner to a Tennis Dessert Party, it's easy to build a theme around your most memorable moments. Ask each person to remember their most memorable moment during the year. Script the entertainment to be the sport's highlights of the year, with a sportscaster narrating the evening, and featuring each team member.

Love Match © A dedicated tennis player wanted to throw a memorable party for her team members. All year long she saved tennis ball cans and filled them with candy. She added each person's name on a sticker on the can that designated an award for that player—from "Most Improved" to "Super Server."

Spirit Days

Spirit days are one of the most fun things about high school, and certainly the most memorable since you have a chance to make yourself look like a fool and score points for it! Whether you sell chances to participate for a few dollars, or do something outrageous (but in good taste) to get attention from the local media, here are some ideas that have created many memories throughout time.

- Hat Day
- Bad Hair Day
- Mismatch Day
- Backwards Day
- Pajama Party

* Junk Food Day
* Giant Chocolate Chip Cookie Day
* Car Wash Day

The Cheer Of The Year ⓒ We've Got Spirit . . . Can You Hear It? Have a schoolwide contest to develop the best cheer on earth. Announce a "cheering" talent show. Each cheer must be presented in front of the students at an assembly or special evening. Students vote on which cheer they like best, and the most spirited cheer and favorite amongst the students will become the cheer of the year and sounded at every upcoming game!

The Good Luck Tree ⓒ In front of the office at one high school, a very large artificial tree held wishes for the players. Students wrote "good luck," "go team" messages on slips of paper and attached them to the tree. Before every game, the tree was filled.

Team Parents

A Night Out ⓒ Your Team Mom (or Dad) worked hard. They deserve a night out sponsored by the team. Collect a certain amount from each player, and put together a small suitcase with all the necessities for a night out. From a gift certificate to a nearby restaurant to movie passes and a slew of snacks, indulge them with a break from the hard work that accompanies being a team player's team parent!

No One Can Hold A Candle ⓒ If you are the Team Mom, and you want to thank all the other parents for their help, do what our Team Mom did at our pot-luck end-of-the-year banquet. She gave out a candle to each family and said, "No one can hold a candle to each of you!" As she presented each candle, she commented on what that family contributed during the year to the team. It was very touching and everyone felt thanked from the bottom of her heart.

A Charming Supporter ⓒ For the team parent who is there year after year, purchase a charm bracelet, and add a charm every time you wish to thank her for being a team mom. It's easy to find those charms that are in the shape of the sport—from volleyballs, or soccer balls, to footballs—whatever the sport, add the charm to the bracelet and present the gift at your sports banquet. The key, though, is to compliment the team mom by letting her know how charming having her around has been.

Gifts For The Coach

A Tisket, A Tasket ☺ Fill a basket for road trips and games with bottled water, energy bars, power drinks, super-sized snacks, and more. Add a note that says, "A tisket, a tasket, goodies for the best coach *ever* are in this basket." To top off the basket in a memorable style, give the coach a gift certificate or gift card from the entire team to a favorite sporting goods store or place he or she loves to shop. Don't just think sports if you wish to be memorable, your coach does have a life outside your playing field.

For A Good Sport ☺ Lorie Lewis suggested a great idea for your kid's coaches. Since every town has a sports bar/restaurant that is well-known for attracting sports lovers, give the coach a gift certificate to eat out. Big screen televisions in every corner, game rooms, and great food will be the destination for your well-deserving coach, who is such a good sport.

Give A Holler. Give A Dollar ☺ Celebrate the coach and, instead of giving her something she doesn't need, have everyone on the team attach five one-dollar bills to a Christmas tree by fan-folding the bills, and then wrapping a pipe cleaner around the center of them and attaching them. You can also use a sturdy branch, or a plastic lei that she'll actually put on and wear around her neck. Let her know how priceless she is with this creative gift and the gift of choice.

Just Ask ☺ Be sure to ask your coach, or a special teacher, what her other interests are outside of the sport. They don't just live, eat, and breathe sports (well, maybe some do). This was clearly evidenced when I asked Coach Malloy, a veteran volleyball coach of over twenty years, about her favorite gifts, and she commented, "I collect angels and love anything that has to do with that theme." So, now, we know just what to get Coach Malloy for her team of angels. Anything angel-related.

Good Sports © If your coach is a dedicated tailgater, grill-over, super bowl fan or baseball fanatic, and attends sporting events often (especially his or her particular sport), then consider the gear that suits him or her best. From high-tech binoculars, to a portable grill, to stadium seats, collapsible travel chairs, or the latest cooler with all the bells and whistles, it's easy to shop for someone who loves the thrill of the game.

A Word From The Coach © One team parent recorded all the inspiring and quotable comments her child's beloved coach said at games and while coaching the kids, and had each one painted in the school's colors on a white bench in the coach's honor. It proved to be one of the greatest gifts ever. It also included the coach's name, the players' names, and comments from each one stating what the coach meant to them.

Winning Words © Have a trophy or plaque engraved with an acronym for the word "coach." Here are a few examples, or you could create your own.

Cares about
Others.
Always dedicated.
Cheers us on and
Has a heart of gold.

Thanks to an
Excellent coach.
Always
Making a difference.

W
is for Weddings

A wedding day can be the most meaningful and memorable day in your life. It is also an opportunity to create beautiful and meaningful memories for everyone sharing in this significant occasion. Each of the special events leading up to the big day sets the tone and stage for what's to come, so adding your personal touch to each experience is a gift in itself.

Sue Winner, of Sue Winner & Associates Ltd, who is a master bridal consultant with over two decades of planning magnificent and memorable weddings, commented, "After coordinating thousands of weddings throughout the years, the one thing that makes a wedding really memorable is when a bride pays attention to the guest's total comfort. When a bride says it's *her* day, she misses the boat. Certainly, it's her day, but making the day special for others is what makes it really memorable for everyone. Every bride wants something new and different, but the key is to focus on how you can make other people feel really special and appreciated for attending your special occasion."

From the showers, to the ceremony, and wedding gifts that will leave a lasting impression, the following ideas will help you create a memorable "I do!"

Bridal Showers and Parties

Taking The Plunge! © Here's a fabulous party that's especially fun when you have a bride or groom with a sense of humor. Make a huge splash with your guests by having a bath (and linen) shower. Since the theme is centered on "taking the plunge," it's also adaptable to a bride, or groom, or couple who is getting married for the second time. Bath showers are popular, with gift items like his-and-her monogrammed towels. Specify the bride's colors on the invitation to help make it even more memorable. Shower favors include shower caps, bubble bath, bath gels, bath soaps, or hand towels.

Honey Do Shower ◎ Help the bride get her future hubby—aka "honey"—in line and ready to fix things, do errands, replace light bulbs, and you name it. Call it a *Honey Do Shower*, and shower the bride with a Honey Do List, and all the accessories that should accompany it: light bulbs, tools, picture hanger kit, etc.

Surprise Shower ◎ Here's a memorable idea for any bride: give her one less thing to worry about or even think about, and invite her to a surprise shower. Don't tell her a thing, and arrange the entire shower with her only knowing that it's a surprise and no details are available! Send the bride her own invitation that says "SUR-PRISE . . . A shower is being given for you. Showing up is all that you'll do! Bring your beautiful smile, _____ is the date. Arrive at _____ and don't dare be late!" Assign one person (perhaps her mother or a best friend) to pick her up, blindfold her, and get her to the party on time!

She's Got Mail ◎ If you want to have guests bring a gift, but don't want to focus on having the bride open the gifts at the party, a fun shower, especially for someone who is combining two households, or starting a second marriage, is a gift card or gift certificate shower. Ask each person to put their gift card/certificate in an envelope, and then present all the envelopes to her in a handpainted colorful mailbox you purchase at a hardware or home store, and add the couple's address and name to it for a special keepsake.

Around The Yard Shower ◎ They now have their very first backyard and, instead of an around-the-clock shower, have an around-the-yard shower. From grilling to chilling out, gifts can include anything that has to do with the great, big, beautiful outdoors. You could also ask family members to bring the bride an exotic or unique plant that could be used in their new home, or planted in their backyard, and use them as the centerpieces at the party.

A Flower Shower ◎ One bride was showered with advice about flowers. Since that's a huge part of the wedding—from the bouquet to the centerpieces, and more—here's an idea that family and friends of one bride who adores flowers gave her when she got engaged. The theme was "Flower Power," and each person brought information and a sample of a flower to the shower—a flower that was in season during the time the bride was getting married, and a few fun facts they researched about it.

Sinfully Good Party ◎ When we say sinful, we mean sinfully good (not bad!), and so we leave that job to none other than chocolate. Have an indulgent party, and serve every imaginable form of chocolate so that it's really over the top, and totally memorable. Friends of the bride and groom could bring something chocolate and the recipe to go with it if they baked it. Give the bride a recipe book that's blank and, when guests arrive, attach their recipe to a page in the book.

A Girl's Night Out ◎ Out-rageous that is! Plan a special dinner and then have a Pajama Party. The entrance fee to get in the party is the secret ingredient—you have to bring loads of *junk food*!

Life Is A Game ◎ Have a shower and invite guests to bring something for the bride and groom that is fun—from games, to gift certificates to the movies, to anything that adds fun and games into their lives.

Pocketbook Shower ◎ Some brides really prefer gift certificates to their favorite stores, and this works when inviting really close friends and family who won't think you're too presumptuous to ask. Another fun game to play at this shower is called pocketbook surprise. Throughout the shower ask if anyone has certain items in their purse (like a pair of pliers, a purple comb, or even a sandwich) and the first person to claim "I do" wins a special door prize like a purse comb, mirror, or loads of breath mints (purse-sized, of course).

A Shower Of Happy Tears ◎ A Connecticut bride, Alison-Catherine Hylenski, recalls a memorable shower given by her mother, Angela, and sister, Kristen. "My bridal shower was such a hit, with over forty of my closest friends and family members present and enough scrumptious Italian cuisine to feed a small army. My aunt Judy said a prayer over the day and over my marriage that brought a tear to every eye. As one of the "bridal shower games" my sister asked me to explain ten reasons why I love my fiancé, Shawn (another tear-jerker). As I listed the reasons, a bridesmaid wrote each down in gold writing on a piece of paper and put them into a keepsake. Everyone who never had the pleasure of meeting my fiancé got to learn why I've chosen him as my lifelong mate. My sister incorporated a recipe exchange, whereby each shower guest was given a stamped envelope with my new address, and asked to go home that day and send me their favorite family recipe. She presented me with my own recipe box to hold all of the recipes that would soon arrive in the mail. What an unforgettable day it was!"

Pre-Wedding Gifts And Bridesmaids'/Groomsmen's Gifts

Engaged! © I love to give an engagement gift that commemorates the date a couple got engaged. Record the date and have it engraved, or etched, into a lovely keepsake. For example, have a clock engraved with the quote *Today is a gift, that's why they call it the present.* Below that, list the couple's names and engagement date.

Tickled Pink © Let the couple know that you're tickled pink to hear their good news, and send a beautiful floral arrangement, or a nosegay of assorted pink flowers. Add a note that says, *We are tickled pink to hear your news. Congratulations on your engagement!*

If Friends Were Flowers © For a very special bridesmaid for whom you want to do something really extra special, or your maid or matron of honor, take a picture of a flower you'll be carrying in your bouquet, and enlarge and frame it so it's really beautiful, just like your friendship. On the back of the framed print, add a note that says, *If friends were flowers, I'd surely pick you!*

Picture-Perfect Groomsmen © Guys are often content with cufflinks, money clips, or personalized gadgets, but to make your gift more memorable, give him a copy of the earliest photo you can find of the two of you. On the back of the frame, write "A picture-perfect friendship, best buds forever," and the date. Another gift that was memorable was from a groom who selected famous quotes that he really felt fit each of his groomsmen. He had each quote engraved on a block of silver to be used as a paperweight. On the back of each of the paperweights was the date of the wedding and a sentiment from him. The choice of words was so meaningful, and so fitting for each individual person, that, over twenty-five years later, his groomsmen still tell him they have those paperweights on their desks.

Who's Who © Here's a memorable thing that one mother-in-law did for her daughter-in-law—when she made her list for the wedding of all the friends and family members her daughter-in-law would be meeting, she wrote something special about each of the people on the list, something that was personal and related to her son. For example, if a close friend helped his dad move him into his first apartment, it was noted. Or, if someone gave him his first job, or wrote a recommendation letter for his college application, that was listed. It gave the bride such a wonderful insight into who was who!

Flower Girl And Ring Bearer Gifts © If you are having children in your wedding, consider inviting them in a memorable way. Think out of the box and come up with an idea that they will relate to. Have a giant cookie invite them in frosting. Personalize a cake, "Will you be my flower girl?" Make it fun. One couple asked their ring bearer to be their super "wedding hero" with a favorite superhero they made holding a little pillow and toy ring. Another couple asked their flower girl with a bouquet of lollipops, and a wedding dress costume for her to wear for Halloween, and to get in the spirit.

Welcome Bags

A Six-Pack Welcome © A southern bride created a clever welcome gift for her out-of-town guests staying at the hotel by recycling Coca-Cola six-pack holders. She had her friends and family save them for a solid year, and then used the six-pack holders instead of a welcome bag. She filled them with goodies, and a small can of Coke, juices, and bottled water, and wrapped each six-pack up with clear cellophane, a brightly colored ribbon, and a note that said, "It's the real thing—Susie and Randy, July 20th, 2002. Welcome to our wedding weekend."

A Welcomed Tote ◎ When selecting a welcome bag, think of something practical that your guests will actually enjoy and use after the wedding. Consider selecting something like a fabulous tote bag with their name on it (put your name and wedding date on items inside the bag or on a hang tag) for a more personalized and thoughtful gift that they'll carry later. Then get creative and reflect a theme. One bride and groom who loved to jog selected a health food focus, and filled the bag with healthy snacks, fruit, and bottled water. The water bottles had their name and wedding date on it, plus, "H_2O . . . Happy 2gether!"

Tips To Make Your Wedding Memorable ◎ Sue Winner, master bridal consultant, suggests the following tips for making your wedding memorable:

- Make your wedding memorable for your guests. Go around to every table and thank them for coming. Expressing your gratitude to every guest is the key.

- Music needs to be quieter while people are eating so they can hear one another.

- Consider something special at each place setting. For example, instead of using chair covers, one bride put a little bouquet of wildflowers for the guest to take home on the back of each chair. It looked beautiful and was very unique.

- Personalize your wedding to reflect your interests. One bride's mother-in-law collected antique quilts, and the bride requested that they be the underlining for tablecloths. Of course, an actual tablecloth topped the quilt to avoid anything spilling on it, but it was a very cozy feeling.

- Add special touches to each stage of the wedding. To add sentiment to her special day, one bride used her mother's headpiece and veil to surround the wedding cake. It was bunched up around the cake, and a beautiful touch.

- Instead of the traditional white aisle runner, consider using rose petals, unless your dress has a long train which will sweep the petals.

• If you are giving out favors, do something that has lasting value. One bride and groom gave a small tree sapling to plant in honor of their union.

Weddings With Pizzazz

Picture This ⊚ One bride and groom set up two beautiful chairs covered in white satin, and instead of having their photographer take their photo standing at every table, each table was invited to surround the bride and groom at their chairs of honor, and have their group photograph taken there. Not only was it memorable, but the guests enjoyed a variation on the dinner table photograph.

A Snippet Of Love ⊚ We recently attended a wedding and discovered a memorable story that will live on in our hearts forever. Our friend Ken, the father of the bride, tells it best. "After my wife Brenda's mother, the ever spunky Grandma Betty Siegel, ninety-three, died suddenly on January 17th, 2002, Brenda was sorting her belongings and found the dress that she had worn to our wedding in 1963. Attached was a small note—clipped with one of those old-fashioned wooden clothespins—in Grandma's handwriting, identifying its history. The sense of profound loss that we were feeling was heightened when, just a few weeks later, John, our son-in-law-to-be, proposed to our daughter Suzanne, and they set a wedding date for the following October. As plans evolved, Suzanne, Jenny (her sister/maid of honor), and Brenda began looking for wedding gowns, as well as dresses for themselves. Brenda took Grandma's dress out of the closet in our home and hung it on the door of our bedroom. She tried it on but it didn't work. Jenny tried the dress on with the same result. And Brenda kept saying to all of us, 'I can't believe that Grandma's not going to be at Suzanne and John's wedding.' One night, around 3 or 4 A.M. as a nervous mother of the bride tends to do, Brenda awoke, took down the hem of Grandma Betty's dress, and snipped off a 3-or 4-inch piece of the fabric. In the morning, she called Suzanne at her office, and told her that she'd figured out how Grandma could be at the wedding—referring to the fabric fragment. Since Grandma always liked to be at the center of the action, an idea had been hatched. The swatch was taken to the designer of the gown and sewn into the hem. So Grandma walked down the aisle, joined the ceremony, and danced the night away at her granddaughter's wedding, adding an element of private joy for those of us in on the secret. The gown is now safely in storage, with Grandma's snippet still in place."

Bouquets To Remember © Rebecca Carter, a bride who wanted to make her bouquet really special, spent eight months beading tiny pearls into flowers. She learned how to do this age-old craft, and then even wired her graduation pearls as the center flowers. Her bouquet of pearls was the most striking bouquet that anyone had ever seen. In the "something old and something new" tradition, she also wanted to add something old to her floral masterpiece, so she added a cameo pin to it, as a reminder of her beloved grandmother who had recently passed away.

Sweet Dreams © Here's one memorable detail at a recent wedding that stood out in the guests' minds. After the wedding, as guests were waiting for their cars, a cookie table with coffee and hot chocolate was set up for a last-minute memory. This was a crowd-pleaser, since the guests anticipated a long line, and this was certainly a sweet way to say goodnight.

The Wishing Well © Create a memorable way to wish the happy couple well with a little wishing well. Search for either a small replica of a wishing well, or a pretty basket with the handle wrapped in ribbons. Place slips of pretty paper by the well, attach a pen to the handle, and add a sign.

Have some advice?
For the couple—do tell.
Please write and place it in
The wishing well.

To Your Good Fortune © Wish a bride and groom good luck, as they journey ahead, with a symbol of good luck. Cindy Simmons shared an idea that her best friend had had for her and her husband's wedding day. She placed money in a silver fortune cookie with a special note. To this day, Cindy has the fortune cookie sitting on her desk as a reminder of her friend's thoughtful wishes, and a sign of good luck. You could also do this with a four-leaf clover, a shiny new "lucky" penny, or any other symbol for good fortune and enduring happiness.

Something Old, Something New, Something Mom, Something You ©
Your family heirlooms can become an important part of your special day, just as they were a part of your mom's. Recently, one bride used the dress worn by her mother and three aunts, since she was the first of her generation to get married. Yet the dress was not her style, so she incorporated it into the ceremony by detaching the train from the dress and draping it over the altar. Her sister, who is getting married next month, is also using the train, and they plan to pass it around to all the cousins. It's a major family heirloom.

A Box Of Bliss © Create a lasting treasure for the bride and groom by purchasing a shadow box and filling it with memories from the wedding. Paste the invitation inside the box, and surround it with other special mementos—paper napkins with their names, a photo you took at the reception of their wedding cake, or other little details, like the food, dried flowers from a centerpiece, a favor box, or bag of bird seed. You can even request the garter from the person who catches it. The key to making this gift spectacular is to accumulate things that the bride and groom won't have the presence of mind to think to gather and save.

Something Old © One very sentimental mother saved for many years the Bible she carried down the aisle, so that when her daughter got married, she could carry it as well. Not only did she have three girls, but now many generations and daughters later, the same treasured Bible has been carried down the aisle at over one dozen weddings.

Midnight Breakfast © One couple, who planned to party at their wedding into the wee hours of the evening, had a breakfast hour that debuted at midnight. A special room opened that was adjoined to the ballroom, and it was transformed as the couples' Breakfast Diner. It looked like a diner, and the smell of coffee filled the room. They served waffles, French toast, omelettes, bagels, breakfast pastries, doughnuts, loads of coffee, and all the toppings.

Falling Leaves © If you are getting married in the fall, a lovely touch is to provide buckets of faux or silk-like leaves available from a craft store or florist. They make a gorgeous display when thrown at the bride and groom as they depart from the wedding and look beautiful in the photographs. Plus, they are reusable and easy to clean up.

Memorable Wedding Gifts

A Wedding To Remember © Jack Morton, of Indulgence Salon, suggested one of the memorable wedding gifts that he gives a bride and groom. Jack shared, "Since the bride and groom so often don't get to taste everything, or really enjoy the food at their own wedding, I like to give them a picnic backpack that includes containers for food, utensils, etc., and have their married name personalized on it. However, the key to this gift is that it includes instructions to give it to the caterer before the wedding to pack up with samples of everything for an after-the-wedding feast, just in case they are hungry. I include a bottle of wine, and put in linen napkins for a festive touch, and a note that says, "Only open when you are Mr. and Mrs." On the note inside I write a personal message and end it with, "Hoping your life together is picnic perfect!"

The Best Gift Ever © Amanda Perkins faced a difficult challenge months before her wedding, since her mother passed away due to a long illness. Right after her mother's funeral, Amanda's three cousins wanted to do something meaningful to lift the burden of the wedding plans off Amanda's shoulders, and they offered the best gift of all. They requested the honor of taking care of her entire reception. Amanda, stunned, was so touched, and this lifted the weight of the world off her shoulders, and meant so much to her. Since they were quite experienced at catering and doing parties, they took charge, incorporated all of Amanda's requests, and did all the cooking, baking, and centerpieces. Amanda said, "It was the best gift anyone could have ever given me."

Then And Now © An ideal gift for a bride and groom to give to each of their parents is a double-sided frame. On one side have a photograph of you and your mom when you were little, and save the other side for a photograph of you and your mom at your wedding. The gift of "then and now" will be special and memorable.

Invitation Sensation © Don't overlook the wedding invitation, since it's a sensational way to preserve a memory for the bride and groom. The wedding invitation presents itself as the ideal gift, one you could give back in a new and creative way. Consider re-creating the invitation in another medium, such as having the content painted on a ceramic plate by an artist, and fired, embroidered on a wall hanging in their favorite colors, embroidered on a silk pillowcase, created as a tapestry (which is what one bride did), or suspended in a beautiful antique or modern frame, depending on the couple's taste.

It's Their Choice! © When you don't know what to give, a pre-paid gift card or gift certificate to a store the bride and groom are registered at is a wonderful choice. Add a poem to your card like this one:

Please enjoy this gift with all our love,
Wishing you endless smiles and laughter.
Select something that you really need and want . . .
And may you live happily ever after!

Clearly Meant For Each Other © When giving a wedding gift that is crystal, a beautiful cut-glass pitcher, or anything that's totally clear, add a note to your gift that says, *It's totally clear—the two of you were meant for each other!*

Happiness sneaks in a door
you didn't know you left open.
—John Barrymore

X

is for X-tra Challenging People and X-tra Special Ones, Too!

She's x-tra special and you really want to go all out and do something memorable. He's your favorite uncle, and you just can't see getting him any old thing, it has to be perfect. Or, leave it to Dad . . . he always says he wants nothing, needs nothing (except you), and is quite a challenge. Now what?

Those special people in our lives are one of a kind and deserve the most memorable gifts of all. But how do you find something that will reflect your love, appreciation, and gratitude for the role they play in your life? And how do you choose a gift for someone who won't give you a clue, doesn't want a thing, or returns everything you give because he or she doesn't need or like it.

Gifted givers have unlimited resources and figure out way ahead of an occasion what to purchase. They act like Sherlock Holmes and do their job. In my book *The Giftionary: An A to Z Reference Guide For Solving Your Gift Giving Dilemmas . . . Forever!,* I presented an A to Z listing of endless gifts for you to choose from. Here's some assistance, however, just in case you still don't know what to give.

Gift Giving For X-tra Special Challenges

* Begin by considering their gift-giving personality. Yes, that's right, gift personality. Does she value donations to a worthy cause, senti-

mental gifts, or does she love to be indulged with jewelry? In order to really please someone, you must know what she or he really wants, appreciates, and prefers. Once you fully understand their definition of the "perfect" gift, then you can rise to the occasion.

- Start researching what he or she wants months or weeks in advance. If you procrastinate and wait until the last minute, you'll make your gift-giving search really stressful. Ask them about the worst gift they've ever been given, what they don't want, or have too many of, and you'll get them talking. Then try and probe them for answers to what they really admire, want, or need.

- Now snoop! That's right. Snoop. This might take time, the help of a mate, secretary, favorite salesperson, friend, or your own investigation, but it's possible to please even the most difficult person on earth.

- Purchase the gift ahead of time and save the receipt, or get a gift receipt from the store. Giving the gift of being able to return something is a memorable gift in itself. Be super creative and write a *permission-to-return* poem like:

I searched for something special for you,
But just in case this gift doesn't do,
Please do me the honor and take it back—
I want you to be happy and that's a fact!

VIP (Very Important Presents!) For X-Tra Special People

Accountant ©

You're Number One. Find a bronze or crystal number one . . . a paperweight, or carved plaque. Or, how about something else to crunch besides numbers? Send some indulgent toffee, or delicious snacks.

Aunt ©

Dear Aunt Perfection. This sounds wild, but it is really memorable. Write a letter to your aunt and tell her why she's perfect. Here's a sample:

Dear Aunt _____:

If I searched the world over for an aunt who was totally perfect, I would instantly be led to your door. And, what a lucky girl I am that _____ years ago, when I entered the world, I was given a rare and special gift. This gift was so perfect that I could hardly believe my good fortune. And that gift was you, Aunt _____. You are my perfect aunt for so many reasons, but let me share a few. (Now, you finish the rest!)

Brother-In-Law ©

Take Care Of The Details. If your brother-in-law is always helping you with the details, like mine is, give him the gift of detailing, and send someone professional to detail his car. You could also give him a year's worth of car washes, if he's a car lover. Thank him for taking care of life's little details!

Clergy ©

The Gift Of Inspiration. Write a letter to your minister, preacher, or rabbi, and make a donation to his or her favorite cause. Tell him how he is a shining example that inspires you to be a better person every day.

Dad ©

Bar None, The Best! If you know a wine connoisseur, or someone who enjoys a well-appointed bar, fill it up with personalized items, like bar towels with their initials or name. From personalized cocktail napkins, to engraved silver bottle-stoppers, to custom labels for their wine that you can even make on your computer (if you're savvy), there are so many ways you can let someone know that "bar none . . . they are the best!"

Doorman, Housekeeper, Or Community Helper ©

Collection To Perfection. The best gift to give someone who will be getting loads of little gifts is to group your building, clients, or customers together, and collect a specific sum of money, and give the individual a great big whopping check to spend anywhere, anytime, on anything he or she so desires. Put the check in a pretty box and wrap it up with all the bells and whistles.

Family Member ©

Faraway Family. If you have a family member or friend who lives in another city, send something special that's famous in your hometown. For example, in Georgia, peaches are plentiful, so peach preserves could be a peachy-keen gift. Or, do what our cousin Harriette from Florida did. She sent the juiciest oranges ever, from an orchard near her house. With a little investigation, you'll find loads of hometown favorites.

Father-In-Law ©

Blast From The Past. Your father-in-law might be difficult to shop for, but it's easy to find something to please him if you return to his past. All you have to do is find out what car he drove when he was a young man, or investigate a restaurant or someplace he frequented in the past. Then take him back to a blast from his past by visiting the restaurant, if it's still standing, renting, for the day, the actual car he drove, or getting together a few of his fishing buddies or best friends, and treating them all to lunch.

Friend ©

Take Note! One of my favorite gifts of all time to give a friend was shown to me by my close friend Meredith Bernstein. It's called a jotter. It's a little leather notepad that fits in the palm of your hand and provides a smooth writing surface. The front of the jotter has corners, which hold your paper in place, and there's also a place in the center of it to store additional paper. It fits in your purse or briefcase, and takes up little to no room, since it's flat, and is an ideal gift for anyone on the go. It's a handy organizer that lets you write on it easily, jot a note, and stay organized in the process. I can't do without mine, and it's a memorable gift for anyone, especially a friend!

Count On An Orchid. When in doubt, it works every time. Have a florist prepare, in the fine tradition of florists, a beautiful orchid in a pretty pot with all the trimmings—curly willow pebbles, or moss to cover the roots—and have it delivered. This is a favorite flower for a favorite friend, since it's easy to take care of, lasts a long time and, like your friend, it's beautiful inside and out!

On The Record. If everything you tell your best buddy is "off the record," give him or her a fabulous record, or CD, of a hot group you know he or she loves. Add a note that says, *On the record, you're the best friend on earth.*

Godparents ©

One Of A Kind. Godparents have no expectations when it comes to gifts, but a nice thing to do is to thank them for their time, attention, and concern for you or your child's well-being. Give a godmother a "fairy godmother award" by having a magic wand placed in a cake, or thank a godfather with a plaque that says:

As godfathers go,
You're second to none.
Thanks for your caring
And thanks for the fun!
Presented with love and appreciation, _____

Grandmother ©

A Gift To Treasure. Here's a really meaningful gift for a grandparent, and then your entire family. If you enjoy scrap-booking (or if not, and you're still game to try your hand at it), and have the patience and time, then consider an out-of-the-box gift that will keep on giving to both your grandparents, and everyone later on. If your grandmother or grandfather have photographs they've collected throughout the years piled high in overflowing storage boxes, give them a large box, gift-wrapped, with a note inside that says, "This gift entitles you to one magnificent scrapbook. *Please fill this box with pictures you treasure. In one month will return a gift that's my pleasure!"*

Grandfather ©

A Cell-a-bration For Grandpa. Here's what one family did for their grandfather to help him stay in touch when he was out and about. They purchased a cell phone for him, gave him lessons, wrote down how to use it, placed the directions in large letters on a laminated card that went in his wallet, and then programmed emergency numbers and numbers for everyone in the family in the address book. Now, every year, they pay his cell phone bill, since he loves calling all the grandchildren and checking in.

Hairdresser ©

Personalize It! Hairdressers get more baskets and bottles of wine than they know what to do with, and that's not to say they don't enjoy them, but consider a more personal gift for them by having something customized with their name or initials on it, or give them the gift of choice with a pre-paid gift card, or gift certificate to their favorite restaurant for two. Or, invite them to a special dinner to toast his or her talents. Since my hairdresser, Jack Morton, adores his dogs beyond words, I decided to give him a portrait created from a recent picture he had just taken of the dogs—with Santa caps on their heads. There are many companies that will do this for you. You just have to be sure that you take a non-copyrighted picture, or a snapshot you take yourself, and you can have them enlarged, or even painted on canvas. I framed the portrait, and it's now one of his prized possessions, hanging over the mantelpiece.

Mom ©

Display Your Affection. Place an ad in a community newspaper, or your church, synagogue, or religious affiliation's newsletter, stating your love for your mother. Display your affection in a creative way. Here's one idea: *we're big on love but short on space, Phyllis Freedman we adore your face! With love, your devoted children.*

Sweet Remembrances. For years, I've saved the card that was attached to beautiful pink roses and chocolates, that my son sent me from college thousands of miles away, surprising me with them one Mother's Day. The words are what sweetened the gift, since the card said *Mom, you are as sweet as these chocolates and as beautiful as these roses. I love you. See you in a few hours. Justin.*

A Perfect Day. One favorite gift of all time was the day my husband and our kids gave me a perfect day. Every mom will love this gift, but you have to prepare to be really attentive. Here's how it works: Begin by creating a menu of choices for Mom, and call it Mom's Menu For A Perfect Day. Include places to go for breakfast (including breakfast in bed) lunch, dinner, and then a list of chores, activities, and things to do. Give Mom the menu the evening before so she can pick everything she wants, including the time she wakes up! Begin her day with a smile and tuck her in at night. Don't forget choices like bedtime stories, hot tea or milk, and cookies, and all the trimmings. This will be one day she never, ever forgets. It will be perfect, just like you!

Mother-In-Law ©

If You Were A Flower. Give your mother-in-law the ultimate compliment and a gift to remember. Take a picture of a flower that perhaps she's sent you, or one that you carried (or she carried), in a wedding bouquet. Enlarge it and have it matted. Leave a space to sign the photograph, and sign it with the phrase *If mothers-in-law were flowers, I'd surely pick you! Love,* _____.

Neighbor ©

Neighbors In The Know. Collect and save an assortment of coupons, take-out menus, great baby-sitters, and resources in your neighborhood that you use and appreciate, and put all the contact information in a colorful tote bag. Add a note that says, *Knock, knock. Who's there? The Johnsons are . . . Any time you need us!*

Nurse, Dental Hygienist, or Physician's Assistant ©

The Gift Of Choice. If you wish to thank a nurse, hygienist, or physician's assistant, consider writing a note to their boss stating how wonderful their care was during your recent visits. Giving praise to their boss is an especially positive and memorable thing you can do. It takes time and energy, but will be a very memorable deed. When it comes to gifts, take a moment to learn about their interests, or if they have children, and select something that can be brought home to the family and enjoyed, like a gift card to a video rental store, a home-baked goody, or a copy of a wonderful book you recommend.

Unsung Heroes. The people who labor in doctors' offices and hospitals, quietly doing their work—these are the unsung heroes of the healthcare system and they deserve your thanks. Tell them you want to sing their praises with a gift of music. A pair of tickets to a concert, along with a gift certificate for dinner and a CD, will sing your thanks. Another gift that hits the spot is a gift certificate for spa services (their aching backs and feet will thank you). Or, here are some suggestions from dental hygienist Gail Heyman: "I have been given such lovely gifts over the years, which have ranged from lunch invitations where you get to know someone better, a pretty toothbrush holder (perfect gift for a hygienist), or a visit to their workplace if their line of work was fascinating."

Music Teacher, Tutor, or Coach ©

Take Note. While piano teachers love teaching music, they've been inundated with mugs with musical notes on them, so consider something more personal. If the teacher taught your child to play a particular instrument, sport, or otherwise, give them the gift of play as well. A gift certificate to a nearby restaurant, or local mall, will be music to their ears. Add a thank-you note "singing" their praises.

Postman ©

Here's A Smart Tip! While recently at the hairdresser, the postman stopped by the salon to deliver the mail. I asked him what the nicest thing anyone had done for him to say thank you for a job well done, and he recalled a deed yesterday that meant the world to him. He explained, "I was delivering a package to a man who didn't speak much English, and he wasn't home. I had to go to the office, and back and forth to his apartment, to find him. He finally answered the door at home, and was so pleased that I didn't leave without delivering his package that he tipped me. He couldn't have imagined how much that meant to me, since yesterday I was actually down to my last dollar and really needed it."

Service Helpers ©

At Your Service. Turn the table on someone who has served you really well, and let him or her know you're at his or her service. Give him or her something really indulgent. If she cleans your home, how about some indulgent hand creams, a manicure, and a gift certificate for a massage. Or a gift certificate to a fabulous store she's admired, presenting her with the gift of choice. If he is the best mechanic on earth, find out his favorite car, and fill a basket with favorite foods from the country that car originates in. Or, give him an evening out to a nearby restaurant for two or, if he has kids, shower them with toy model cars, and gift certificates to video stores.

Sister ©

A Tale Of Two Sisters. Anne Dennington's sister, Bitsy, surprised her with a book that chronicled their childhood as well as all the trips they had taken throughout the years. She called it *A Tale of Two Sisters,* and it became one of the most memorable gifts Anne had ever received. From Greenville, to New York, to Jackson Hole, Italy, New Zealand, and England, it was filled with photographs, stories about their life together, and details about the many journeys they've shared as sisters.

Sister Act. Since your sister is the best ever, create an acronym, or special phrase, for your sister, and have it written in calligraphy in a pretty script, or print it out on the computer, and frame it. You could also do this with her name. Here's an example using the word "Sister":

Such an
Incredible
Supportive
Terrific person who means
Everything to me and I
Really adore you!

Sister-In-Law ©

A Sensational Sister. If your sister-in-law is really a sister to you, just like mine is, then let her know with gifts that say "sister." There are endless books, charms, and lovely gifts that spell it out. Or, give her a heart of gold, and add this note:

Since you married our brother,
We think he's quite smart,
To have chosen someone as special as you,
Who now lives in our hearts.

Teens ©

A Gift To Flip Over. Teens love flip-flops, so give her a gift that she'll totally flip over. Search for flip-flops in a variety of colors and styles, and fill a hanging shoe bag for a clever presentation, and tell her no one can fill her shoes! Include a manicure and pedicure for a gift that is a step in the right direction.

Uncle ©

Brief Him On Your Love. We recently sent my uncle a briefcase that was filled with his favorite goodies, and he really loved it. Our note read, "We just wanted to brief you on how much we love you." His thank-you note was priceless, and reflected our gift. It read, "Thanks very much for your terrific gift. *Briefly*, I appreciate your thoughtfulness. With love, Uncle Jerry."

Tutor ©

Thank You Merlin. Has he worked magic with your child, helping him to improve his scores, his skills, and increase his knowledge? Then tell him he's worked magic, by appearing with something he really is interested in—from a favorite hobby, to a magazine you know he'd enjoy. That's easy to find out, since your child can do the asking. Or, do a little investigating, and find out his favorite food, and bring a picnic basket filled with it for a little R&R on an evening off. He deserves it!

Realtor ©

To A Real–tor Star. Give your favorite Realtor a piece of surreal real estate by having a star named after her. Send a star map showing her star with a card, *To the best Realtor in the universe.*
Make a plaque for your Realtor with an inscribed poem:

My Realtor has a magic touch
With houses, condos, property, and such.
Not only does she have a heart of gold . . .
But everything she touches turns to "sold!"

Secretary ©

You're Number One. Once a year is not nearly often enough to tell your secretary how special she is. Make it a tradition to honor her on the first day of each month, telling her each time, "You're number one." A perfect fresh flower on her desk, a gift certificate for dinner, theater tickets, a gift card to her favorite store—go overboard occasionally, and let her know what a great job she's doing.

Teacher ©

A Favorite Purse-n-ality. All women have handbag preferences. Observe what type of purse your child's teacher carries. Is it a shoulder bag, hand-held bag, black or brown, and does it snap or zip? With a little research, you can select the perfect handbag and tell her she's your "Favorite purse-n-ality" and a super teacher.

Volunteer ©

Heart Of Gold. The best way to thank a volunteer, a teacher, or leader of any kind who has tirelessly worked for a good cause is to give him or her a "heart of gold." This could be a gold heart pin, tie tack, necklace, or even a paperweight. You can also search for one by visiting a gift outlet that sells paperweights, or desk accessories, and if you can't find a gold heart, have it etched into a brass wall plaque with the honoree's name. If you are on a strict budget, you could have one drawn by a child, covered in gold glitter and framed. Add the sentiment, "To someone with a heart of gold. We treasure you!"

Loving Cup. Purchase a trophy and have it engraved with the volunteer's name and a quote, or the phrase: A loving cup for a caring heart. Fill the cup with chocolate kisses and add a note that says "Our cup runneth over, thanks to you."

Y

is for You Don't Know What To Give or, You Don't Have Time!

Y ou don't have time? Time isn't on your side? We've all been there and felt that shortage of time—that's for sure—but you don't have to have lots of time to add your signature style and personal touch. Creative gift-givers, party planners, and effortless entertainers have lots of tricks of the trade up their sleeves, and you can, too. In fact, you'll be amazed at how little time it takes when you have a few versatile gifts on hand when you don't know what to give. The key to success in making it memorable when there's just no time to do so, is to have loads of options and creative ideas at your fingertips.

This chapter arrives to your rescue! Whether you're shopping for the hard-to-please—those family and friends who are impossible to figure out and return everything you get—or you want to add your personal touch in a jiffy, you've come to the right place. The key is to figure out a few gifts you really enjoy giving, and then stock up. There's no substitute in this area for getting organized and planning ahead. Be prepared to give those gifts, and have the necessary materials on hand to get the job done.

My favorite suggestion of all time if you want success is to designate a drawer or area and call it a gift closet. If you already have a gift closet in place for those gifts for gift-giving emergencies, then you know who you are, and way to go! You're constantly thinking about being thoughtful, and you always have something on hand that would bring a smile to someone's face. However, for the gift-giving– and party-impaired, here's help to get you started. Every gift closet needs a variety of items, but there are some basics and staples that will help you prepare for those gift-giving emergencies, especially when you need a gift and don't have time. This chapter will help you prepare for being memorable, but keep in mind that, no matter what you give, you can make it meaningful in a positive way and avoid giving items no one needs or wants!

How To Create And Stock Up A Gift Closet

Once you designate an area that will serve as your gift closet—even if it's a drawer, or a clear hanging clothing bag in a closet—then you're on your way. Even if you have limited space, you can install a few extra shelves, or find a box that slides under the bed to store gifts. No excuses! Begin by stocking up on items that relate to the specific interests of the people you give gifts to often or that are in the style in which you enjoy entertaining.

- Be prepared by having greeting cards for all occasions on hand. Stock up on colorful stamps that you enjoy using, a few colorful pens, and stickers to jazz up your envelopes. Also have on hand a variety of gift bags in different sizes, gift-wrapping paper that would lend itself to a variety of occasions, clear tape, and scissors. If you're computer-friendly, use mailing labels, and create gift stickers that say, "A Gift From The _____" Print a few pages to have on hand. That way, you're instantly prepared to wrap it up and go.

- Think of the occasions you need gifts for often. Hostess gifts? Thank-yous for your child's teachers? Birthday presents for the birthday-party circuit your kids are on? Involve your kids and family and select a few to have on hand that you'd be delighted to receive and give. Pre-wrap them when you have time, or make sure the bags you have fit them, for a grab-it-and-go gift.

- Stock up on plenty of pre-paid gift cards, certificates, movie passes, and those favorite books that would appeal to anyone. These take up very little room. Also, have some subscription cards that pull out of your favorite magazines, and record those online resources for ordering gifts that can be delivered in minutes.

- Think like a kid. Don't forget those unexpected friends who drop in with their children (no-mess art projects or kits are great for those occasions), or all the baby gifts you need to send. Have a few little "I love yous" and games to help out when you have to give a gift in a flash. Select items that lend themselves to wider age groups like a children's book that's a classic, or a game that's suited for all ages.

- When you get a gift that's memorable, take note and consider what's in your gift closet that's really special and, in keeping with this book and making memories, be sure to stock up on those memory-making opportunities.

- And last, but not least, keep on hand entertaining accessories like personalized cocktail napkins, colorful placemats, an instant centerpiece that doubles as an accessory when it's not in use, party mints, birthday candles, place cards, candles, and other ways to add instant pizzazz to a party.

Gifts To Choose From

Sign Of The Times ☺ Frame up some choice words. Begin by thinking of the quote or adage that best fits the person to whom you are giving this gift. In less than ten minutes, you can measure a frame's opening, type the quote, pop it right into the frame and—viola! If you are computer-savvy, transfer the quote into a savvy font, print it out, and pop it into the frame and—viola! If you don't have a computer, or you want to be really creative, cut out the letters that make up the phrase from a magazine and collage your quote. You can be inspiring, funny, quote their favorite saying, and get your point across in style. These quotable remarks, and memorable signs, will become the most memorable gifts ever, and will be enjoyed for years to come. Refer to the chapter "Q is for Quotes," but here are some other ideas to get you started.

Remember Your A, B, C's . . . **A**lways **B**elieve you **C**an do it!

No Good Deed Goes Unpunished!

MVP—Most Valuable Parent

Do Not Enter! Mood Swings In Progress

What Goes Around Comes Around

There's No Other Like My Mother!

Daddy–O—How I Love You–O!

Friend On Call—(your telephone #)

Forget Love—I'd Rather Fall In Chocolate!

Paper Moon ◎ Whenever I don't know what to give someone, or I want to give something really useful, I always think of stationery, and pretty paper in colorful patterns and styles—from little blank books, to notepads, to personalized stationery (if there's time) with an icon that matches the person's interests. You can also transform a blank page into a meaningful gift by adding someone's name and address, and you can customize stationery on your computer. When it comes to paper, the sky is the limit!

Create Your Own Gift Certificate ◎ Too often, we lack the time to do each other the favors we would really benefit from and appreciate. Enter you! Give a gift certificate for a personal service like a massage, baby-sitting, or whatever you do well that your friend would really enjoy. Give the gift of your talent, whether you are a super organizer, a great baker, cook, or a gardener extraordinaire. Don't underestimate your time or your talents. This gift really delivers!

Give Some Time Out! ◎ You might not be able to give him or her more hours in a given day, but you can give a well-deserved break. Purchase a gift certificate to a favorite restaurant, or tickets to an event he/she will enjoy. Add a small clock, or watch, to let them know it's time to take her out for a fun night alone. Or, just give him or her the day off to do whatever he or she wants.

Minute-Made Gifts On The Go ◎ There are many fabulous gifts that can be purchased in seconds. Here's how to make it memorable, and it all happens in less than ten minutes at your grocery store. Go to a store that has a bakery, and have a cake instantly personalized while you wait. Then, select a magazine from the magazine department that fits his or her interests, and place it in a gift bag from the wrapping-paper aisle. Pull out the subscription card and send it as soon as you can. This minute-made gift will make you look like you spent loads of time and effort and will really be enjoyed.

Mirror, Mirror, Off The Wall ◎ Whenever I don't have time to be creative, or don't know what to give, I give a magnifying mirror. If someone travels a great deal, I give a travel-sized one, for other times, a super-magnifier that sits on a vanity and doesn't let you miss a wrinkle. These gifts are a great choice, and I add a note that says, "Mirror, mirror, off the wall, Hope your birthday is a ball."

Emergency Beauty Kit ◎ One of my favorite ideas came from a woman who loves to buy makeup kits on sale, or whenever she sees them, and keep them on hand, ready for gift-giving emergencies. She fills each kit up with on-the-go travel-sized beauty supplies, ranging from a nail file, to little samples of hand lotion, face wash pads, perfume samples, a few bandages, a purse-sized comb, a quarter for a telephone call, to a small compact mirror, and a lipstick. Her beauty kits have reigned as one of the favorite gifts she ever gives, and she always keeps a few on hand in case she needs a gift. Inside each one, she adds a few quotes about beauty, like: "If beauty is only skin deep, then what do we need all this for?"

Phone Cards ◎ Phone cards are easy to find and simple to give. They fit right into a greeting card and are available at most every drug and grocery store. When someone you know is traveling overseas, or moving away from friends and family, phone cards are always a time-tested gift where you just can't go wrong. Include a picture of your family, or group of friends, and add a note that says, *When you miss your home sweet home, call us soon on the telephone!*

Super Solutions ◎ OK. You saw it on TV, and at a friend's house, and you tried it, and it really, really worked for you. When you discover a gadget you love, then consider stocking up on a few and giving those "tried-first and true" gifts to others. From the latest dicer to the latest slicer, once you discover a fabulous gadget, have a few at your fingertips when you just don't know what to give. What makes this so memorable is that they've seen it a hundred times and wondered if it really works. Add your testimonial on your note.

I love this gadget,
It worked for me,
I hope your favorite,
It will be!

Freezer Pleaser ◎ If he loves frozen pizzas, or a particular flavor of popsicles, or is a cake, or ice cream lover, purchase an assortment of freezer goodies, and fill up his freezer with items that will please him. If you know what flavor ice cream they love, go overboard and get a dozen pints. *Chill out and enjoy these goodies.*

Something In Style ◎ When you don't know what to give, select something in style. If pink is the hot new color, or baby blue, stick to a basic accessory, like a wool scarf (if she lives in a cold climate), or a belt, in the hot new color. Include a fashion magazine that has the hottest trends and include a note that says, *Inside this gift is a great big smile, for someone who is always in style.*

Special Delivery ◎ If you want to give a gift that the entire family will appreciate, give a gift certificate to a take-out restaurant that delivers. Pick up the gift certificate and a take-out menu. Wrap it up by rolling the menu around the certificate and tie it off with a ribbon. Add a note that says, *A special delivery just for you, to thank your family for all you do!*

DV Delight ◎ Stock up on a few of the classic movies now available on DVD. Combine them with some popcorn and candy for an instant hit! Add a note that says, "Hope this gift DVDelights you!"

It is one of the most beautiul
compensations of this life that no
man can sincerely try to help
another without helping himself.
—Ralph Waldo Emerson

Z

is for Zero-cost and

Low-cost Ideas

Save the best for last! Z is for zero-cost and low-cost gifts and winds up *Make It Memorable* on a cost-saving note. That's right, gifts that cost very little. In fact, some of the best gifts you'll ever give and receive are totally free, or very inexpensive. They also are so memorable, and can really touch someone's heart. The good news is, there are endless zero-cost and low-cost gifts that provide lasting value. It's not how much you spend on a gift that makes it memorable; it's whether or not your presence is included in the present.

When we give of our time, talents, wisdom, and even our connections, we offer a piece of ourselves. There are so many things we can do to help one another, and this chapter illustrates a variety of ways that you, too, can give gifts that are zero-cost or low-cost, but still create special memories, and help you bond with those friends and family you so adore.

This chapter addresses how to spend little, but get big results!

To Grandma's House We Go © One of my grandparents' favorite gifts in the world was just a visit. My grandmother's face would light up when we would show up. One night, while out with friends, we decided to go and visit my grandmother, and then drive over and stop and visit with one of their grandparents. We called ahead to forewarn each, and then took turns learning about each other's family history. It was a gift we gave each other as friends, and didn't cost a thing, but was a priceless memory we still talk about and treasure.

Recycled Greetings © Whenever you receive a colorful greeting card, cut off the front of the card, if the other side hasn't been written on, and recycle it. You'll find that these secondhand cards become new greeting cards with a renewed life. You can use them as hang tags for gift packages, or fold them over for clever notes.

Tag. You're It! © Next time you receive a note from someone special, and he or she wrote it on their personalized stationery, cut off the personalized part of the card that has their name, initials and/or address on it, and save it. Purchase inexpensive, but colorful luggage tags at an office supply store, and slide their name right into the tag. Or, you can actually cut out the part that's pretty, laminate it, punch a hole and tie a ribbon onto it, and transform it into a work of art that can't be missed when they are trying to spot their luggage.

Coupon Surprise © Everyone knows that coupons are free and often fabulous. But, next time you're shopping, here's a thoughtful idea you can do for a friend, that will be such a surprise, and only cost you a little time. Ask around at your favorite store's customer service department, or the concierge stand at the mall, if they provide any special shopping coupons, or incentives for shopping. Most of them do provide coupons, free magazines, maps, and other services you'll find surprising. Get some for yourself, and also an extra set for your friend. Fill a small shopping bag with the coupons from the store and add a bright ribbon. Not only will this gift be free, but your friend will think you went to great lengths to be thoughtful.

Manicure Magic © A lovely thing you can do for someone, that is low in cost, is to offer a manicure. This is especially meaningful for a senior citizen, or someone who is confined to bed. From a massage to a simple change of polish, this deed, which costs very little, will be memorable and heartfelt. You'll also make someone feel really special and a bit more glamorous!

Emergency Card © Here's a little idea that is a really meaningful gift for your family. Type up all your critical telephone numbers, including your family's cell phone numbers, your insurance agent, physician's numbers, and other very important telephone numbers. Laminate it at a quick-copy store and create a list for each family member. In an emergency, make sure everyone knows who to call, how to reach them, and their back-up numbers.

A Shard Of Glass ◎ I was particularly touched by a story I heard, about a woman who combs the beaches every year collecting shards of broken glass that have been tossed in the ocean, and survived the waves, and ferocious storms. When they wash up on the beach, she collects the prettiest ones, cleans them up, and saves them as year-round gifts. She places the shards in little bottles, or just places them in small pretty gift boxes. She adds a little personalized note to each one to make her gift more inspiring and meaningful. For example, when a close friend of hers was ill, she wrote a note expressing how the piece of glass weathered the storm, was thrown, tossed, and turned, yet it came out even more beautiful than ever. She added that she hoped, and knew, her friend would, too.

A Singing Telephone Call ◎ Have a friend with a wonderful voice? Enlist his or her help, and schedule a telephone call to your recipient, and say it's from you. Choose a song that fits the occasion, from The Beatles' "Birthday" (and use a kazoo for sound effects), to "I Just Called To Say I Love You." For a friend who is newly divorced, send "Tomorrow" (the sun will come up tomorrow) from the musical *Annie*. You're bound to get an instant thank-you, and your singing phone call will be very memorable.

"Just Count On Me" Coupon ◎ Create a coupon on your computer, write it in a greeting card, or just create one on paper, and call it a "Just Count On Me" coupon. The coupon is redeemable for a shoulder, errand-running, or listening ear. Give your friend a book of them, or a single coupon, and send them often, especially when you know someone is having a tough time and might need to know someone cares.

Talent Exchange ◎ Have a friend who wishes she could dance, and you move like Fred Astaire? One who wants to play that piano in her living room, and you play like Liberace? What about the guy who can't cook, and your friends call you Julia Child? Or, he wants to play tennis, and you play like McEnroe? Offer your time to teach whatever your friend wants to learn. You will get to spend quality time together, and he or she will learn something they always wanted to know how to do. For example, if you play the piano, teach your partner to play, and if he's a great golfer, then he could exchange the favor and get you up to par. This is a wonderful idea to extend to a friend or family member who admires your special talents and you admire theirs.

A Visit Back In Time © She or he has a wealth of memories, so tap into them! A really memorable idea is to give someone a remarkable blast from the past. Don't tell them one detail about whatever you arrange, and see if you can coordinate your own little elementary or high school reunion, with a few of her favorite friends, or a teacher she adored. Do a little research about his or her favorite childhood memory, book, place to eat as a child, favorite elementary school friend, and then arrange the experience. Perhaps a visit or call from her seventh-grade teacher on her birthday, a visit to the library to check out her favorite book from childhood, or a visit to the exact playground that she grew up playing in. This will take a little effort, but re-creating a beloved memory will add a nostalgic touch that will be greatly appreciated.

The Photo Box © Here's a gift that will require endless hours of time, but be one of the most memorable gifts you'll ever give. Give a friend a pretty box, and wrap the lid of the box separately, so that it can be lifted off and on without disturbing the wrapping. Add a note that says, "This is your life! The enclosed coupon entitles you to the ultimate gift to preserve those special family memories. Please fill this box with tons of photographs that you'd like to have assembled into a special scrapbook. In one month, your gift will come true."

Give A Mailbox Coupon © Give a neighbor you'd like to help a standing "mailbox coupon," good for bringing in their mail when they are out of town, or for plant-watering, or anything else they might need. While this is usually a given, it's such a nice deed to remind them that you are standing by to help, in any way, at any time.

Season's Greetings © Every year, have your kids invite friends, and other kids in the neighborhood, to come over for a holiday greeting card party to design their greeting cards. This is such a fun activity, and they will love making their own cards by recycling pieces of greeting cards you saved, and designing cards to give to their own family. These personalized cards made by kids will become special treasures throughout the year. Plus, everyone will appreciate you organizing this thoughtful activity.

Garage Sale Party © Team up with another family and have a garage sale party. That's right! The kids will have the time of their lives. Decide whose garage the sale will be at, and then encourage the kids to join you in cleaning out your house. Hang a shopping bag in every closet weeks ahead of the sale, and begin filling it up with items you no longer wear or want. Involve the kids by assisting them in setting up a lemonade stand, and allow them to make some money off their sales for a savings account, or a good cause. Another fun incentive is to let them each buy something from the other family (with your permission). Not only will this day cost you very little but, while it's hard work, you'll enjoy each other's company, and clean out your house as well.

Celebrate An Unsung Hero © For many years, I wrote a volunteer column featuring community members who are good Samaritans and unsung heroes. It was one of the most memorable things I ever did, and I discovered how many opportunities there are to put the spotlight on others. You don't have to be a columnist to sing the praises of an unsung hero and, with a few phone calls and a little persistence, you can make it happen if you know a deserving soul. Perhaps there's a friend, child, family member, or even a neighbor or teacher who has done something worthwhile for a good cause, or accomplished a huge feat that deserves attention. Let the media know, put the spotlight on them, and call your local newspaper editor, or television station, and suggest they do a story on them. If they really don't want the media attention, then write a special letter to commend them on their efforts.

A Year Of Reminders © During a particularly difficult year, one woman gave her best friend a special gift. She called it "a year of reminders." She knew her friend, who had just lost her father, was really preoccupied, and might forget important dates and other special occasions, so she gave her the gift of reminding her about all the little things—like calling a family member, or friend, on their birthday, or congratulating others on special events, or just good times to save money on sales. This was one of the nicest things she could have ever done, and for years they have made an agreement to reciprocate with each other, and constantly remind each other all year long.

A "Centimental" Gift ◎ Show someone special your appreciation with a gift that will keep on appreciating . . . a mint-condition penny, or a penny from the year he or she was born. Add a note that says, *You're Cent-sational!*

Good Luck ◎ Give someone a symbol that wishes him good luck. This might take a little time to find, but good-luck signs are all around us. Perhaps give him a piece of wood to knock on next time he needs good luck, or what about a four-leaf clover that you search for and find in a clover patch in your backyard? Or, if you find a lucky penny, pick it up and give it to a special friend for good luck! These gifts that wish someone well will be so memorable, and just might bring him some good luck to boot.

Personalize A Picture Book ◎ Have an inexpensive, worn-out picture book lying around, and want to bring it back to life for a young child to enjoy? Do what one mother did with a used copy of *Old MacDonald*. She wrote, with a black pen, her child's name throughout the book, instead of Old MacDonald. Instead of Old MacDonald having a farm, it read "Blake Austin had a farm . . . E–I–E–I–O." Her child loved his own version of Old MacDonald, and it became such a favorite of his that she had to read it every night for well over a year.

Check It Out! ◎ Take a child to your public library and help him or her apply for library card. Include regular visits for checking out books and encourage a love of reading.

Always be a little kinder

than necessary.

—James M. Barrie

Make It Memorable VIP Record

**Favorite family traditions, recipes, and other details
I wish to preserve and continue**

_____

_____

_____

_____

_____

_____

_____

_____

_____

_____

Most memorable books

_____

_____

_____

_____

_____

_____

_____

_____

_____

Most memorable on-line shopping sites

_____

_____

_____

_____

_____

_____

_____

_____

Favorite 1–800 numbers, or sources

_____

_____

_____

_____

_____

_____

_____

_____

Make It Memorable VIP Gift List

Name

Telephone & e-mail address

Mailing address

Birthday and other special days

Sizes, likes & dislikes

Hobbies & special interests

Previous gifts given

Previous gifts received

Name

Telephone & e-mail address

Mailing address

Birthday and other special days

Sizes, likes & dislikes

Hobbies & special interests

Previous gifts given

Previous gifts received

Name

Telephone & e-mail address

Mailing address

Birthday and other special days

Sizes, likes & dislikes

Hobbies & special interests

Previous gifts given

Previous gifts received

Name

Telephone & e-mail address

Mailing address

Birthday and other special days

Sizes, likes & dislikes

Hobbies & special interests

Previous gifts given

Previous gifts received

Name

Telephone & e-mail address

Mailing address

Birthday and other special days

Sizes, likes & dislikes

Hobbies & special interests

Previous gifts given

Previous gifts received

Name

Telephone & e-mail address

Mailing address

Birthday and other special days

Sizes, likes & dislikes

Hobbies & special interests

Previous gifts given

Previous gifts received

Name

Telephone & e-mail address

Mailing address

Birthday and other special days

Sizes, likes & dislikes

Hobbies & special interests

Previous gifts given

Previous gifts received

Name

Telephone & e-mail address

Mailing address

Birthday and other special days

Sizes, likes & dislikes

Hobbies & special interests

Previous gifts given

Previous gifts received

Name

Telephone & e-mail address

Mailing address

Birthday and other special days

Sizes, likes & dislikes

Hobbies & special interests

Previous gifts given

Previous gifts received

Name

Telephone & e-mail address

Mailing address

Birthday and other special days

Sizes, likes & dislikes

Hobbies & special interests

Previous gifts given

Previous gifts received

Name

Telephone & e-mail address

Mailing address

Birthday and other special days

Sizes, likes & dislikes

Hobbies & special interests

Previous gifts given

Previous gifts received

Name

Telephone & e-mail address

Mailing address

Birthday and other special days

Sizes, likes & dislikes

Hobbies & special interests

Previous gifts given

Previous gifts received

Name

Telephone e-mail address

Mailing address

Birthday and other special days

Sizes, likes & dislikes

Hobbies & special interests

Previous gifts given

Previous gifts received

Name

Telephone & e-mail address

Mailing address

Birthday and other special days

Sizes, likes & dislikes

Hobbies & special interests

Previous gifts given

Previous gifts received

Name

Telephone & e-mail address

Mailing address

Birthday and other special days

Sizes, likes & dislikes

Hobbies & special interests

Previous gifts given

Previous gifts received

Name

Telephone & e-mail address

Mailing address

Birthday and other special days

Sizes, likes & dislikes

Hobbies & special interests

Previous gifts given

Previous gifts received

Name

Telephone e-mail address

Mailing address

Birthday and other special days

Sizes, likes & dislikes

Hobbies & special interests

Previous gifts given

Previous gifts received

Name

Telephone & e-mail address

Mailing address

Birthday and other special days

Sizes, likes & dislikes

Hobbies & special interests

Previous gifts given

Previous gifts received

Name

Telephone & e-mail address

Mailing address

Birthday and other special days

Sizes, likes & dislikes

Hobbies & special interests

Previous gifts given

Previous gifts received

Index

Veterans' Day, 148
volunteer, gifts for, 199

Washington, Booker T., 170
wedding favors, 45–46
wedding invitation, 188
weddings
    bridal showers and parties, 178–81
    bridesmaids' gift, 181
    flower girl/ring bearer gifts, 182
    groomsmen's gifts, 181–82
    memorable gifts, 187–88
    mother-in-law gift to daughter-in-law, 182
    pre-wedding gifts, 181
    welcome bags, 182–84
    with pizzazz, 184–87

welcome bags, 182–84
When Bad Things Happen to Good People
    (audiocassette), 99
Women For Hire: The Ultimate Guide to Getting
    a Job (Johnson/Spizman), 50
words at work, 169
work
    gifts and deeds at, 111–15
workplace parties, 109–15
    gifts and deeds, 111–15
    National Boss's Day, 147
    Secretary's Day, 143

Yom Kippur, 146

zodiac signs, 15

Other Books By Robyn Freedman Spizman

The Giftionary: An A-Z Reference Guide for Solving Your Gift-Giving Dilemmas . . . Forever!

When Words Matter Most: Thoughtful Words and Deeds to Express Just the Right Thing at Just the Right Time

The Thank You Book: Hundreds of Clever, Meaningful, and Purposeful Ways to Say Thank You

Women For Hire: The Ultimate Guide to Getting a Job
(with Tory Johnson and Lindsey Pollak)

Women For Hire's Get-Ahead Guide to Career Success
(with Tory Johnson)

Getting Through to Your Kids
(with Dr. Michael Popkin)

A Hero in Every Heart
(with H. Jackson Brown, Jr.)

Life's Little Instruction Book for Incurable Romantics
(with H. Jackson Brown, Jr.)

Getting Organized

Quick Tips for Busy People

Kids on Board

Monsters Under the Bed and Other Childhood Fears
(with Drs. Stephen and Marianne Garber)

Good Behavior
(with Drs. Stephen and Marianne Garber)

Beyond Ritalin
(with Drs. Stephen and Marianne Garber)

If Your Child Is Hyperactive, Inattentive, Impulsive, Distractible: Helping the ADD/Hyperactive Child
(with Drs. Stephen and Marianne Garber)

www.robynspizman.com